COME
THE NEW
JERUSALEM

John Michael
SHERDON

Blue Pearl Unlimited

Copyright © 2000 John Michael Sherdon
All Rights Reserved.

Published by Blue Pearl Unlimited
P.O. Box 777, Amityville, NY 11701
Orders: www.johnofthelight.com

ISBN: 0-9661942-0-9

Library of Congress Catalog Card Number: 99-095368

Front cover and text illustrations: John B. Sherdon

Printed in the United States of America

5 4 3 2 1

Dedication

*This book is dedicated to those who have
ears to hear and eyes to see,
for the glory of the Father cometh.*

Acknowledgments

This project has taken almost ten years to complete. Some special thanks are in order. I would like to thank my girls for their constant support: my wife Diane, my daughter Sara, and my mother Frances (87 years young). I'd like to thank my son, John, for his artistic gifts and for our "special relationship." I'd like to thank the ones who've assisted me on the content of the manuscript: Peter, Jeannie, Joan, and my publisher, Paul Clemens, for urging me to do more than the original entry. Lastly I would like to thank my friend and brother, Jesus, and all the members of the Ascended Host, especially: Mary, St. Germaine, White Eagle, Buddha, Paramahansa Yogananda, Babaji, Swami Nityananda, Swami Muktananda, Gurumayi, and St. Fiacra (the patron saint of gardeners), for their upliftment and constant friendly needling. And, of course, Yahweh, The Ancient One, The Great I Am That I Am, for being the source of this amazing spiritual journey for us all.

Table of Contents

Introduction	1
Part I Prelude	3
My Story	5
How to Use This Book	10
The New Jerusalem (The Vision)	13
The Anointing	16
Part II Body (Temple)	19
The Breath As a Tool	21
A Fit and Healthy Temple	23
The Three Ds: Discipline, Determination and Dedication	27
Sexuality: Obstacle or Pathway?	30
Fasting	32
Part III Practical Life	35
Inner Vision	37
What is True Success?	40
Serving God on the Job	42
Be a Victor, Not a Victim	44
To Gain the World and Lose Your Soul	46

Laughter, the Greatest Therapy of All	48
The Lesson of the Butterfly	50
Change: A Necessity for Growth	53
Why the Earth Changes?	55
Non-Doership	58
Honor Thy Mother and Father	61
Teach Your Children Well	63
Sports Fans—Root for God	65
The Gift of Life	67

Part IV Heart (Seat of Consciousness)	**71**
The Warrior's Heart	73
The Glory of Love	75
Conviction of the Heart	77
Love and Unity	80
We Are One Family in God	82
America—The Torch-Bearer of the Light	84
The Second Birth	87
Joy, the Road to Freedom	90
Seeing with Our Hearts, Not Our Minds	92
The Healing Power of Music and Dance	94
How to Pray Successfully	97
Forgiveness	99
Giving Is Better than Receiving	102
The Role of Womankind in the Golden Age	104
Adversity	107
The Leap of Faith	110
An Open Letter from Jesus	113

Part V Superconscious Mind	**117**
Humility, Not Self-Aggrandizement	119

Self-Forgetfulness	121
Erase Egotism—Give All Credit to the Father	123
Eradicate Fear and Doubt Through Transmutation	125
Meditation—Godly Food	128
Silence	131
Intuition	134
Be as Gentle As a Dove and As Clever As a Serpent	136
Open Minds, Open Hearts	139
The Group Mind Dynamic	141
Give Up Being Right and Be at Peace	143
Illusion Creates Confusion	145
We Are Creating the Apocalypse	147
Channeling: Its Use and Misuse	149
The Role of the Guru	152
United We Stand, Divided We Fall	154
The Attention	157
Part VI Multi-Dimensional Spirit	**161**
Whispers from the Silence	163
Surrender to God's Will	165
Learning to Trust God	167
All Paths Lead to God	169
We Are Not Alone	171
The True Message of Jesus the Christ	173
The Power of the Word	175
God Is the True Messiah	178
Ascension Is for Everyone	180
There Is No Death	182
The Blue Pearl	184

Awaken the Dreamer	*186*
We Are the Heroes We Are Looking For	*189*
We Are the Collective Messiah	*192*
The Proper Application of the Great I AM	*194*
How to Protect Yourself from Negativity	*196*
We Are the Conduits of God's Power	*200*
The Law of One	*202*
A Voice Crying in the Wilderness	*204*
God Is Ecstasy	*206*
The Quickening and Activation of Critical Mass	*208*
Epilogue	*213*
"The Impossible Dream"	*215*

Introduction

THE TIME HAS COME for us to realize our spiritual potential. Bound by thoughts of limitation, we have fallen from our true birthright—to be sons and daughters of our Eternal Father. We limit ourselves because of fear and a lack of trust in there being anything beyond what our senses perceive as the "real world". But is the world of our senses *really* the real world? It is enough to be content with our lives as we perceive them, holding greedily to our possessions, our families and friends?

I don't suggest we ignore what our senses tell us, but that we expand our perception to include the dimension of spirit. If we did, we would find God in everything—from mowing the lawn or going shopping to pursuing the heights of spiritual ecstasy. In whatever we do, it's the Magic Presence that makes each experience come alive.

We were never destined to be beasts of burden, yet hard work is virtually unavoidable in our society. We are expected to earn our daily bread, meet our obligations and die contentedly, knowing we did our best. While this can be fulfilling on many levels, unless we also nurture our spirits while here on earth, we will never unlock our full potential or realize our true purpose—to *conquer* death. Death is only a transition, a change from matter-spirit to spirit-matter in which the immortal part of us, the God-Self within, survives. If we had this knowledge, we could break away from our conditioned fear of death.

But how do we get this knowledge? Our parents may have been too busy, tired, unaware or simply inundated by fear or cultural conditioning to teach us. We sought enlightenment in church, temple, ashram and sanctuary, but only seemed to find dogma, ritual, tradition and maybe a few fleeting experiences of truth. How, then, do we make ourselves fertile earth in which the seed of the Divine Father can grow, moving us in all His ways? How do we feel the ecstasy, the thrill of living, we have read and heard about? Is true and lasting bliss only for the rare few—the saints, the prophets, the mystics—to experience? Of course not! Everlasting joy is for all of us, if we but take the time to explore life with an open and honest heart. It has been said, "The kingdom of heaven lies within." The validation of this statement can be found in each of us.

This book is a guide to light the way for those who are open to the infinite opportunity life offers. For as people discover life, they discover love . . . as they discover love they discover God . . . and as they discover God they discover the unity and perfection of all things. And as they discover this perfection . . . they find themselves forever.

PART I

Prelude

My Story

I REALIZED THAT ALL THROUGH MY LIFE there was a spiritual knowingness within me. My knowledge of the spirit lay submerged and waited to be awakened. My awakening was catalyzed by a deep personal tragedy. My best friend Lester and my father John passed over just a year apart. Lester was like a brother, since we were intellectually, athletically, socially and spiritually compatible. The impact of Lester's death prompted me to question myself about the meaning of life. I found myself asking this question on a deeper level than ever before.

The summer after his passing, I took a trip cross-country. During that trip, I experienced my first profound spiritual experience. I stood at the edge of the Grand Canyon and there I entered a glorious state of blissful silence. I remained in that state of bliss for over half an hour.

When I returned to my home on Long Island, I began to take classes in raja yoga and eastern philosophy. The disciplines of twice daily meditation, yoga postures, a strict vegetarian diet, and a weekly fast created the atmosphere for my greater awakening.

I had practiced these spiritual disciplines for eight months when my father was stricken with a series of heart attacks. My father passed over at age sixty. My father and I had always been very close. We shared going to baseball games, football games, and other sporting events. We also enjoyed fishing together every weekend. I know how lucky I am to have experienced the love of my family. We did many things together and we shared a bond of love that laid the foundation of my spiritual life and created the protection for my spiritual journey. My dad's passing made me realize instantly that Life must exist beyond the physical body. I began my quest to find the spirit within me that is immortal.

After four years of diligent practice in daily spiritual discipline, I experienced full divine consciousness. It was during the evening in the yoga center, where my teacher at that time gave her lectures. I was expected to sing a devotional chant with my fellow students at the lecture that evening. I was very apprehensive about singing in front of a lot of people. That day I felt wave after wave of anxiety and I began to think up creative ways to avoid showing up. I was giving myself a pretty hard time when suddenly I heard a voice say, "You are going!" The voice was so powerful and authoritative that it startled me and captured my attention at the same time. Needless to say, my agitation diminished and I appeared at the center that evening at a semi-calm state.

As we began to sing the chant, the words on the page of music began to move. I began to feel an energy awakening in my spine. I then became a silent witness. The song was being performed through me. In a state of ecstasy, I wept tears of joy. This new part of me had emerged at the most unexpected moment. I had opened the lid to the superconscious. The whole experience was remarkable, but the evening's events had only begun.

It was my duty to close the center after the lecture. I approached the flame of consciousness on my knees, as I had done countless times. This time, I was immersed in bliss and serene peace. My body was energized from head to foot. I sensed that something exceedingly profound was about to happen. Then, Jesus' words came to me. "When you are empty, you shall be filled." A moment later, the energy of the holy spirit shot up through my spine. The energy shot through the top of my head, lifting me off the ground, tumbling me backwards, and propelling me into the superconscious state. I lay on the floor immersed in divine nectar. After some time, I collected myself and closed the center.

I walked to my teacher's house nearby in that state of expanded consciousness. She took one look at me, laughed, and then exulted, "You know what you want!" While we sat conversing in my new state of awareness, I sensed my body as being beyond its form. Indeed, my attention was now at the level of being one with everything. High-sky lightning was flashing and the full moon was dancing behind the clouds on this warm August night. My consciousness was so expanded that the lightning seemed to pass through my chest. My teacher's husband remarked, "You seem to have a lot on your mind." I replied that there wasn't a single thought in my mind. I saw my mind as a computer that was receiving, sending, and storing data. But the real me, the real life within, was truly one with everything.

I was driven home because I was too Godly-intoxicated to handle my automobile. I slept the yogi's sleep, resting completely yet not sleeping. My body was electrified. The energy was intensified in my crown chakra, giving the sensation of wearing a hat or a crown. I thought of the Hebrew yarmulke and the Indian headdress came to mind as ancient mystical symbols of the fulfillment of divine energy residing in the top of my head. That state of extraordinary awareness lasted over three days and hastened my progress dramatically.

I became accustomed to operating with more of my channels working and I began to teach and lecture at the center. In my search for truth I devoured the Bhagavad Gita, the Upanishads, the Vedas, and the writings of various Indian saints. My search for truth was insatiable and I read anything I could get my hands on.

When my training at the center was complete in 1982, I met the Indian saint Baba Muktananda. I absorbed his teaching without conversation. We never spoke, since his English was minimal. My connection with him was wholly internal. This was a blessing because there was no personal attachment. I achieved that which I set out to accomplish. I awakened awareness of the unstruck sound, the OM, the I AM. I hear it as a sound within my consciousness. Not with the auditory sense, but with the inner ear of spirit. I visually awakened to the light, the Blue Pearl, which is the representation of our soul living within a house as tiny as a mustard seed. Within this seed lies worlds and universes and the totality of our existence. Also, I awakened to extended vision, which is seeing your light amplified through your third eye, onto the field of your experience.

I spent about four years with Muktananda, continuing to teach meditation and right living, lecturing, and counselling people individually to help them to see their light. It was during this time that I encountered an unexpected shift in my emphasis of my teaching. I was experiencing an Easter raja yoga meditation at the New York Whole Life Expo and listening to the music of Kitaro. Then I came upon a large picture of Jesus and Saint-Germaine adjacent to the Logo of the I AM Presence. I stood there transfixed, as if I couldn't move. I remained in that spot for more than half an hour, feeling a deep communion with both of them. It was as if Jesus and Saint-Germaine were opening another door for me. I knew then that my Eastern tutelage was complete.

I opened up to the teaching of Saint-Germaine via Godfrey Ray King, the Bible, and the gift of all gifts, *The Keys of Enoch: The Book of Knowledge*, by J. J. Hurtak. Holding *The Keys* the first time evoked a memory and opened me up to the Divine Mind. The still, small voice spoke and said, "Your mind is my mind. Our thoughts are one. Together we will bring about this change in my people." Since that time, I have had many experiences and communions with both Jesus and Saint-Germaine.

My soul's purpose began to crystallize. As I was in session with my wife and her friend, I felt my energy being funneled out of me and I saw the vision of a cross. I actually passed through the cross and became one with Jesus, whose arms were outstretched. As I experienced this Holy Communion, my wife, Diane, expressed that she saw me disappear, leaving behind only my prayer shawl in the place where I had been sitting. Then my countenance changed into that of Jesus as I began to re-materialize. It was a sweet, easy, safe and peaceful journey.

Shortly after this experience, it was revealed to me through vision, and substantiated by reputable channelers, that I am a reincarnation of Elijah, the precursor to John the Baptist. I exist in a Paradise Trinity with Moses and Jesus. My mission is to help create the attitude within people that is necessary for mankind to receive the "New Jerusalem", the Second Coming of Jesus, and the dawning of the Age of Aquarius.

Come the New Jerusalem synthesizes the teaching of the East and the West. In actuality, the teachings are one. The book will help break down the divisions between people. Its goal is to create the receptivity needed to cultivate the seed of the Christ in people, so that Jesus can make His descent into matter along with the other 144, 000 Ascended Masters. Then we can create the Golden Age of Enlightenment on this planet.

How to Use This Book

To fully utilize the tools given in this book, diligently practice the various techniques which appeal to you.

Most of all, practice inner stillness. There are many ways for you to approach God, but all of them point to silence as the key to awakening. Listen deep within your heart to hear the silence that will bring you the presence of your creator. Through true silence you can create the space inside yourself to receive God.

Know and remember that God loves us dearly. In the coming years every person on this planet will be tested to their limit while Mother Earth undergoes cataclysmic physical changes to reclaim herself. During the coming earth changes it will be tempting to doubt ourselves, God, and everyone else for that matter. Hence, it is essential that you build a solid connection to God now. Without doubt, we will experience the bitter cup before we taste the sweet nectar of the New Jerusalem unless we change the collective consciousness of mankind.

Keep clear in your awareness that each of us made commitments with God prior to this incarnation. We knew beforehand what we would be getting into. We are all here to anchor the Light, to serve humankind, to give each other hope and direction.

Consider the wisdom of the adage "Let go...and let God." Let go of your identity with the human part of yourself. The human in us is steeped in doubt, anger, or fear in some form or other. You must root out these negative thoughtforms so that you can embrace the events to come aligned with God's abiding love. Know that only good will ultimately exist and that no effort is made in vain.

To properly use this book, read it through entirely and then keep it by your bed. Read it again and again intuitively. The part you choose will help remind you that God truly is with you at all times. You will experience a quickening of your energy while you hold this book because the knowledge that comes from Source through a messenger acts as a bridge from the finite to the infinite.

Never lose heart. Have faith in yourself and your creator. God loves you in a way the human mind cannot yet comprehend. Trust him. Have faith in him and know that all will be provided. Draw close to the presence of God within yourself. Remember the Vision of the New Jerusalem. No soul is ever lost, so don't mourn loved ones who choose to go back into spirit during the coming years. Be calm. Be poised. Take your stand. Become what you truly are.

The New Jerusalem (The Vision)

"And I John (the Divine), saw the Holy City, New Jerusalem, Coming *Down* From Heaven, prepared as *A Bride Adorned For Her Husband*. And I heard a great voice out of heaven saying, 'Behold The Tabernacle of God is With Men, And He Will Dwell With Them, And They Shall Be His People, And God Himself Shall Be With Them And Be Their God.

" 'And God shall wipe away all tears from their eyes; and there shall be no more death, neither sorrow, nor crying, neither shall there be anymore pain, for the former things are passed away.'

"And he that sat upon the throne said, 'Behold I make all things new.' He said unto me, 'Write, for these words are true and faithful.'

"And he said unto me, 'It is done. I am Alpha and Omega, the beginning and the end. I will give unto him who is athirst of the fountain of the water of life freely.' "

Revelation (21:1-6)

"New Jerusalem, City of: 1. A city cosmos which will be used by the Councils of the Divine Mind to accommodate transitions from the planetary bases of preparation into the complex structure of the cosmos. 2. In the present program of the Lord, the 'House of Israel' in the heavens which unfolds to permit different floor levels of energy to control and direct the passage of souls and entities on different radiation frequencies and quanta. The 'triggering gates' necessary for the implanting of a Paradise experiment and the offering up of the 'Bride and Bridegroom' as peacemakers to other worlds in the passages between the heavens. (Eze. 41, 42, 43.) 3. A prototype city of the Order of Melchizadek marking a baseline on the planet where the interpenetrating cosmic forces of the Brotherhoods can commune in certain planting and harvesting seasons. A model for the ancient City of Melchizadek, Salem, Ursalima, Uru-salim, Jerusalem, etc. In a larger sense, the 'mother city' founded above the world and anchored to the earth by special energies at Yohuallichan, Tlamohuanchan, Tula, Xuchatlapan, etc., in order to teach Man how to develop a 'face' that can speak directly with the 'divinities.' 4. The home of the beloved of the heavens. (Rev. 3:12, Pet. 2:4,5,9; Rev. 14:104)."

> Definition of the "City of New Jerusalem,"
> J.J. Hurtak, *The Keys of Enoch*, p. 593.

"*Let The River Run*,
May all the dreamers wake the nation,
Come the New Jerusalem."

> "Let The River Run", by Carly Simon
> (theme song from *Working Girl*)

MAY THE DREAMER in us all awaken to the reality of the World of God that is coming:

A World full of love, fellowship and peace, free of hate, divisiveness and conflict;

A World quickened into the fifth dimension, in which men and women are no longer beasts of burden;

A World filled with the love of God, and with people living under Him;

A World of infinite beauty, with opportunities for all who obey the Law of One;

A World with no possessions as we known them, but one in which we possess the gifts of the Holy Spirit, the keys to heaven;

A World free of the prejudice, mistrust, shame and divisiveness, created by the false faces of egotism.

And may we become a true People of God:

A People united, attuned to their higher Selves and completely free of limitation;

A People filled with universal knowledge;

A People who have eradicated disease and halted the aging process through the healing powers of spirit;

A People able to precipitate into existence all they need to live on, according to their covenant with God;

A People whose essences are able to travel by "folding space" while their bodies remain motionless;

A People living, breathing and thinking as one, following the one God and honoring Him in all they do.

In order to bring forth the New Jerusalem, we must actualize the collective dream the Father has seeded in our souls. By continuing to seek spirit without compromise, we *will* live this dream!

The Anointing

ALWAYS, GOD IS WITH YOU. His mighty Spirit is within every heartbeat, every breath, every gesture, and every movement. Truly, there is no separation between you and God; the physical and the spiritual cannot be divided. You and God are one. He dwells within you as your own Divine Self.

    This I know: the boundary between oneself and the divine is an illusion. One mid-winter afternoon I was in session with a dear friend. After a while we noticed the presence of a special essence in the meditation room. It seemed to quicken the atmosphere in an extraordinary way. Soon we were bathed by wave upon wave of Love and Light. Now light poured out through the windows into the surrounding air. Just as we were about to speak, Jesus appeared. Lovingly He greeted us both and remarked that He felt entirely at home with His friends. Declaring that it is making His work easier, Jesus thanked me for my efforts and said that my joy and my love for God are truly and deeply appreciated. Further, Jesus said He wished more people would trust God, follow their inner promptings and more than all, would act on their promptings.

    At that point I became all welled-up inside because Jesus so poignantly expressed my own heart. The past few days had been especially trying due to one thing and another. I was unable to write. I was uncertain of the tack of this manuscript, and I felt immobilized by matters in general. But all that dissolved in the presence of my elder brother Jesus. He lovingly placed His hands on my shoulders and gently lifted off my burden.

Just then Moses entered the room. The two of them filled the room with such great Love and Light that I thought my heart would burst. Then Jesus anointed my head with oil. Next He gave me a cup of wine that I drank willingly. I felt thoroughly quickened and charged. The entire room was filled with an unspeakably exquisite glow.

Jesus thoughtfully answered the many questions I asked regarding my personal mission. He stated that there is much work to do and not much time in which to do it. In all matters there should be no delay. We should not allow our human reasoning to overly question and thereby doubt the truth of what we are being shown.

For a while Jesus reminisced with me, recalling how we had walked together through hell and fire. He also noted that things haven't changed much in two thousand years. Many will not believe what He is saying, nor will many believe what Mary has expressed. But these messages are completely true. Similarly, many will not believe that I am John the Baptist reincarnated. Nonetheless, I am to stand firm in the certainty of this truth.

Now the Archangel Michael appeared and presented me with a sword. He declared that I am to be Defender of the Light. Michael instructed me to hold the sword high overhead and proclaim the Glory of God to all mankind. He also stated that we all have this sword and scepter of dominion to be used individually and as a collective army of God's representatives on Earth.

Jesus urges us to open our minds and hearts, that we may receive Him and others of the Ascended Host. We are not to worry about our loved ones during the coming cataclysms. God will take care of all His children. When the appointed time comes, people will be evacuated from the eastern and western coasts by mother ships fifty to five hundred miles in length. Under the command of Lord Ashtar and his legion, these ships are capable of entirely duplicating the earth's atmosphere. One of the largest crafts is called Excalibur. Many souls in the command of the Archangel Michael and Commander Ashtar are presently incarnate and know this is true.

Jesus mentioned again and again that the transmuting force of the universe is Love. In the Aftertime Love will again reign supreme and we will live in the land of milk and honey. He urges you to call on Him and the ascended host directly so that you can begin to transfigure, or build your light body for taking the quantum leap with the rest of mankind who trust the words of their divine brother. Jesus wants to be seen as a brother. As kin, not as the exalted and remote messiah. As Jesus says, there is no separation between the spiritual and the physical. It is joyous and natural to be with our brethren! The feeling is one of great freedom and love.

And when people open their hearts to Love (Truth) we will all inherit The New Jerusalem (The Land of Milk and Honey.) Of course, we need to prepare physically, mentally and spiritually. We must continue to grow through the times ahead. Jesus said that people will gather in communities of Light in preparation for the great event. He instructed me to build such a center. He said all would be provided for, including the location and the finances. The helping hands and loving hearts would be attracted to it by the light in their hearts.

Again and again Jesus asked that you allow God's will to be done through you. Stand firm. Let the ghosts of the past go. Have fun. Finally, He said He loves you and He prays for your greatest good always.

Part II

Body
(Temple)

The Breath As a Tool

An obvious yet easily overlooked gift we all possess is the ability to breathe. The life-force, or "prana" is carried by the breath; the more fully we utilize this force, the better our quality of life. *The breath is our lifeline to God!*

As you read these words, think for a moment about the importance of the breath. Close your eyes and breath deeply, rhythmically. Observe and release your passing thoughts; take a break from your internal dialogue. While focusing your full attention on the breath, feel as if God is breathing you in and out. Continue and your mind will become still and clear. You will connect with another aspect of yourself; this is your Higher Self, or God-Self.

Haven't you noticed your breathing is shallow and contracted when you are nervous? Conversely, it is deep and open when you are at ease. Your spirit flows—you speak more clearly, listen more carefully, concentrate better. Full and rhythmic breathing improves your health, strengthening your heart and feeding your cells more of the energy they need.

Often when we get excited, people will tell us to take a deep breath. What great advice! But we should be aware of our breathing at all times, not just when we are angry or upset. If we pay constant attention to our breathing, we will experience life to the fullest because we will be peacefully centered.

Jesus said, "Empty yourself and you shall be filled with the Holy Spirit." The breath is the key to living this principle.

A beautiful exercise is to consciously inhale joy and light and exhale despair and darkness. As our awareness expands, we reflect God in every action everywhere we go, not just at home during deep meditation.

Read these words with an open mind; practice these techniques and note the changes they bring. If you have already begun, keep at it. For growth is continual, and life is ever expanding, ever fulfilling itself.

A Fit and Healthy Temple

IT IS IMPORTANT TO KEEP PHYSICALLY STRONG. The body is the temple of the soul, and it should be treated accordingly; a weak, toxin-filled body compromises our spiritual practice. When we feel well, we think clearly, and when we think clearly, our attitudes tend to be positive, fostering a sense of peace and well-being.

Good health begins with enjoying plenty of sunshine and fresh air as well as getting adequate amounts of exercise and sleep. We should strive to break our addictions to drugs, alcohol, coffee, cigarettes, junk food, television, sex or any overindulgence that keeps our souls sleeping deeply. Moderation—and in some cases elimination—is needed. These temporary joys will ultimately lead to sorrow; the one true joy can be found in moving toward our birthright of immortality and unlimited freedom in spirit.

When we move the body we still the mind; when we still the body we move the mind. Moderate exercises including light jogging, brisk, meditative walks and enthusiastic sports activities all help to oxygenate the system, remove toxins through perspiration and balance the emotions. On the other hand, when we are lazy, we worry unnecessarily. Arranging for at least some outdoor exercises is a great help to our mental and spiritual well-being. To be in nature and breath fresh air increases the prana, or life-force, circulating through the body. Thus, we are fully energized.

In addition, what we eat is important, for we are what we eat. We should find out which foods work for us and which do not. Each of us has individual needs—just as we are not all supposed to eat meat, we are not all meant to be vegetarians. Moderate diet of fish, fowl, and small amounts of meat, plus whole-grain breads, brown rice, fresh vegetables, fresh water and juices can give many of us the balance we need. A nutritionist may be consulted to help us learn what foods are best for us. If we use common sense and avoid extremes, we can eat with enjoyment and reverence, thanking God for His daily gift of food.

The proper amount of sleep rests us and regenerates our tired, worn-out cells. If possible, we should sleep before midnight and rise at dawn, greeting the new day with prayer or morning meditation. The morning quiet bathes us in the peace and bliss of the Holy Spirit, filling us with a calmness that lasts throughout the day.

While our bodies slumber, however, much other work is being done; our souls travel nightly on journeys that continually broaden our spiritual awareness. Many of these excursions are erased from our conscious minds before we wake so our spiritual work will not interfere in our earthly lives. The spiritual lessons we learn help to bring our souls into balance with our physical and mental natures.

The importance of breaking free from drugs, alcohol, coffee, cigarettes and any stimulant or depressant cannot be over-emphasized. While these substances may offer temporary relief, they hurt far more than they help in the long run. Why should we rely on something outside of ourselves to pep us up or calm us down? The God-energy within, through the flow of our breath, can accomplish either as needed. We need to allow the light of our own souls to illuminate us! God didn't create these substances so that their use would become part of our daily lives. Instead, let us make *God* a part of our daily lives. With Him empowering us, the occasional glass of wine or cup of coffee won't be harmful. There is no moderating the use of cigarettes or dangerous drugs, however—they can only hurt us and are best avoided.

We should also take care to avoid watching too much television. Be selective, choosing only those shows that are stimulating, enjoyable *and* life-enriching. As we evolve spiritually our tastes will change, so we mustn't chastise ourselves for continuing to watch the occasional mindless program. Be aware that television can be a powerful influence, one whose ideology should not be blindly accepted and followed.

Every choice we make affects us. By making choices that result in a healthy body, we create a physical environment in which maximum spiritual growth can take place. When we balance the physical, mental, emotional and spiritual selves, our lives work for us instead of against us. Let us no longer take our bodies for granted, but begin to treat them with the love, respect and care due such a wondrous gift from God.

The Three Ds: Discipline, Determination and Dedication

THREE REQUIREMENTS FOR SUCCESS on the spiritual path are discipline, determination and dedication. These qualities are more important in attaining our spiritual goals than either talent, intelligence or creativity. None of the latter qualities alone will ensure us of success. Instead, they may falsely boost our egos, filling us with pride in all "we" have done. As we evolve spiritually, we attach ourselves less frequently to the fruits of our actions, knowing the Father within us is the active principle. Thus, "The less we do, the more we accomplish." How can we reach the state of spiritual freedom in which we are egoless and filled with the grace, wisdom and love of the Holy Spirit?

First, each of us should have the discipline to honor his or her Magic Presence everyday. Otherwise, we become distracted and unsure. We must continually focus on God, or endlessly repeat the lessons we are here to learn. Once we choose unity with Him as our primary objective, our inner lives will begin to stabilize regardless of the events of our outer lives. This inner peace will give us the strength to cope with any challenge and remain firm in our commitment to God. Through constant discipline, our positive attributes become strong enough to counteract the pull of our lower selves.

Along with discipline, we must practice moderation. Any stringed instrument's strings will break if tightened too tightly, yet the instrument will make no sound if the strings are too loose. It is the proper tightening—the middle tautness—that produces sweet music. So that we might hear God's sweet music, we must learn moderation in all our activities. If we are too regimented, too stiff in our approach to God, we will be more likely to give up the quest, for self-imposed austerity without love becomes merely tedious. However, if we are too haphazard in our approach—meditating once in a while, reading spiritual materials occasionally and remembering God at our convenience—not much progress will be made. By maintaining a position midway between, our spirits can flourish.

We must also be determined to climb the golden staircase to freedom. Determination is the force that drives us on despite adversity. It is a way of focusing our God-power toward a chosen goal and of overcoming obstacles and disappointments. To endure the schoolroom of life, to perceive the underlying meaning in all of life's many faces, we must be determined to serve only God. There can be no compromise in our relationship with the Father; fence-straddling only weakens resolve and ultimately blocks ascent. We must serve God at all costs, knowing anything we might lose in this world is unnecessary baggage and what we gain is immeasurable joy. We must not be discouraged but the tests we endure, for there is no flowery road to glory—all glory is God's.

It is important to dedicate ourselves to the spiritual challenges at hand; how we live will determine the future of this planet and the severity of the earth changes we will endure. We must all recommit to our Creator, dedicating our lives to serving mankind. As we give, we learn to love our brothers and sisters, and all God has made. Let us dedicate ourselves to our Creator by learning to love each other as He so patiently loves us.

Through discipline, determination and dedication, we can overcome any obstacle to God. So let us each begin to use these natural and vital tools to construct an inner world of love. By seeing God everywhere and ourselves in each other, let us also build a collective world undivided by race, creed or nationality.

Sexuality: Obstacle or Pathway?

THERE HAS ALWAYS BEEN DEBATE regarding sexuality and its relationship to spiritual development. Is celibacy the best preparation for God-enlightenment? Can men and women in this day and age get beyond the body and add mind and soul to the sexual union? Is a moderate, God-conscious sexual existence possible?

Monks, ascetics and holy men have practiced celibacy, choosing to redirect the seminal fluid upward in order to reach enlightenment. This practice increases energy and vitality while fostering the inner peace needed to complete the spiritual journey. Single men and women who choose celibacy while walking the spiritual path must be patient; it is not enough to be celibate in body alone, but in mind and heart as well, and this level of discipline takes time to achieve. One must gradually ease into celibacy, since the sex drive is so strong and can distort other areas of life if coldly repressed. For some couples, especially those older couples whose desire for sexual intimacy has waned, celibacy can be a natural choice.

But what is the proper sexual attitude for married couples and for those in relationships who seek the Higher Self while remaining sexually active? Sex can be used in many different ways: for physical pleasure, for the perpetuation of the species through reproduction or for reaching one of the highest forms of Christed love-energy we can experience. Making love using the body forms one kind of union; adding the mind deepens the experience. But in the most profound union, when two become one in body, mind and spirit, sexuality is a pathway to a much higher love—God's love. This level of sexual union is not merely passionate; a complete self-contained universe is created by this joining of yin and yang, of female and male principles. This has long been the secret of tantra-yoga, in which two God-conscious individuals experience spiritual ecstasy through physical union.

To achieve the highest possible sexual union, the physical, mental and spiritual bodies of the couple must be closely aligned. This closeness exists in pairings known as "soulmates" and is even more dramatically expressed in what are called "twin flames". In the book *Soulmates*, Jess Stearns writes, "The twin flame is one's twin or counterpart, cast out of the same aspect of light, usually having the same tendencies or predilection. Then there is the companion soulmate who is more of a goal-directed love partner, and also the karmic soulmate whom we attract to learn some difficult lessons from our past." Because of the intensity of these unions, sexuality grows out of and directly engages spirit. Little or no energy is lost in lovemaking, since love is the clear intent of both partners. For these couples, sexual love is part of the journey home to God.

For unions that are less finely attuned, sexual moderation is the key. People must either temper their desires or they will overdraw their spiritual accounts. Sexual indulgence keeps people rooted to the animal sides of their natures, the sides that keep them spinning on the wheel of death and rebirth. These partners should continually seek the highest love possible, thus rooting their sexuality in spirit.

Sexuality is truly one of God's greatest gifts, and is another means by which we can draw closer to Him. It is our intentions, our attitudes, and the intensity of our love that determine whether sexuality helps or hinders our spiritual growth.

Fasting

To grow closer to God, practice the discipline of fasting. My family used to say I was starving myself while I fasted all day each Sunday. Since I enjoy food it was a little arduous in the beginning, but I stayed with the exercise and learned about its benefits first hand. Little by little I began to feel lighter and more at ease with myself while fasting.

I had fasted weekly for about a year when I experienced my first profound occurrence of heightened spiritual energy. The family had gathered at my sister's home for dinner. I was downstairs peacefully sitting in the den while my sister, my brother-in-law, their children and my mother were eating their meals upstairs. Suddenly a blissful energy started to rise up my spine. Soon I felt wave after wave of this potent energy. It seemed to insulate me in a state of ecstasy for some time. It kept me quite entertained while my family ate dinner.

Presently each member of the family came downstairs and offered a remark or a look that told me they couldn't understand the reason it was so satisfying to deny myself the pleasure of eating. Nonetheless, the energy I experienced gave me great confidence and I began to practice fasting more fervently than before.

My intention was not to set myself apart or to assume a role of superiority by fasting. Rather, I wanted to find out its value for myself.

Fasting prepares you physically, mentally and emotionally to receive more energy into your system. It cleanses and purifies your body, your mind and your emotions, giving you rest from the process of digestion and the elimination of waste materials.

There are many ways to fast. One of the simplest is to drink fruit juice which has been diluted in half with bottled spring water. If you can purchase juice that is free from additives and preservatives, so much the better. Also, drinking bottled water will help to flush your system.

Develop an approach that will help you go through your fast with the minimum of lightheadedness. In the beginning, you could take a teaspoon or two of honey if necessary. Other ways of fasting include water or milk only, and specific juices for specific purposes. After they get used to it, some people fast for several days or more.

The main purpose of fasting is to cleanse the body and thereby help activate the quickening of the spirit. As you release the heaviness of the body, you prepare the space within that allows you to receive your spirit.

The setting that you fast in can dramatically aid the whole exercise. You will feel more meditative and sensitive if you go outdoors into a beautiful natural setting. You can feel, hear, see and smell more acutely when you fast than when you are filled with food.

It is important to eat lightly before and especially after going on a fast. When you break your fast you should eat half the amount of your normal breakfast and then gradually increase the intake of food. Fasting is a wonderful discipline. It can become a joy; not more spiritual castor oil in your life. Once you get used to it, you'll be very glad that you began to fast.

*"Everyone has a power
and it grows when we share it."*

Ferngully (the movie)

Part III

Practical Life

Inner Vision

ABOUT THIRTY YEARS AGO I shared a memorable night on the town with some friends in New York City. After staying overnight I made my way to Pennsylvania Station to catch an early train to Long Island. It was the morning rush hour and dashing commuters were coming in to their jobs from the various suburbs.

As I entered the train station I felt a profound shift in my awareness. In every direction I observed people straining to get to work on time. I felt their tension, their stress, and their sense of preoccupation. Stopping, I asked myself: "Why?" Why do we have to labor like beasts of burden in order to earn our daily bread? Why can't the situation be different? Why can't this world reflect the heavens and be more closely aligned to our true origins?

I asked God and myself these questions when I was barely twenty two years old. I ask them now, three decades later, as a commentary about life in the nineties on Planet Earth. That moment in Pennsylvania Station evoked so much compassion and empathy that afterward my life changed its direction and path. I had been practicing public accounting since 1970, when I was graduated from St. John's University. Now I began to read every book on philosophy and Spirit I could find. The truth moved me deeply, far more than the money I was handling.

One day I began to read *Siddartha*, by Herman Hesse. I read it all the way to work. I was so inspired by it that I continued to read it after arriving at my account in Brooklyn.

I locked the door, piled up the ledgers, and read the book cover to cover until I finished it around mid-afternoon.

Siddartha is the story of a young man who studies truth but is captivated by the world. He leads a worldly life until he becomes disenchanted and disappointed in the world. Ultimately, Siddartha returns to the search for truth and the disciplines of his youth.

Instead of reading this marvelous book I was supposed to be doing my job as the junior accountant. It was my responsibility to accomplish the preliminary work for the senior accountant who would always arrive after two days' time. Now I had less than a day and a quarter left in which to fulfill my obligations. These included a trial balance. Incredibly, every task went smoothly. It was as if a divine hand assisted me. I was able to complete all of my responsibilities including the balancing of millions of dollars on the first attempt just a few moments before the senior walked in. What an experience that was!

A few months later I left accountancy. I became an independent bayman and began to earn my living extracting clams from the waters near my home. The life of a bayman afforded me flexibility and a freer existence with time to seek God and time to study the truth.

If you love God enough you can earn your daily bread without getting caught in the world's many snares. God always has and always will provide the opportunities for us to grow and to discover. As a people, we are now embarking on one of the most challenging, yet most propitious times in the earth's history.

The planet is about to undergo a cleansing and a shift in its orbit. This will prepare us for a Golden Age of enlightenment and peace. This hasn't occurred since the time of Atlantis and Lemuria. But now we are being given time to prepare within.

Follow the vision and the path that is right for you. Establish a closer relationship with God, the Great Provider. Look beyond the imminence of the travail ahead and see the

New Jerusalem in your mind's eye. Hold this vision. Know that life after the earth changes will be one of freedom. People will no longer be bound by the old order of pain and misery.

See the New Spiritual Order. See the Hope of a New Tomorrow. Envision the New Jerusalem! Amen.

What Is True Success?

THERE IS SUCH AN EMPHASIS on success in our society. What is true success? Is it climbing to the top of our chosen fields of endeavor? Is it having beautiful cars, boats, clothes, jewelry and all the other things money can buy? Is it being able to travel to faraway places? Is it having many homes in many different locations, enabling us to always live in an ideal climate?

Society's definition of true success is material gain—a success born of the ego, that greatest of chains binding everyone to the wheel of limitation. This sort of success can be more curse than blessing. God never meant for us to live in poverty, but neither does He want us to take all His gifts and never say "thank you".

"No matter how much money you have, you never have enough," it is said. Just when we think we are financially secure, life throws us a curve. And *then* we remember God, but only to blame Him, to curse Him for our bad luck. Worldly success fades away; all the toil and stress, all the fuss and bother pass in time. But is there a lasting success we can strive for?

When we point ourselves beyond the world of the senses, we see that success is only real and lasting when we give credit where credit is due—to God, the Creator of all things. *God is a sole owner of all we possess!* When we offer everything to Him, we can delight in our earthly gifts and they won't dominate our hearts or make us feel like we've been separated from

Him. But can our egos step aside and allow us to taste true success? Is this kind of surrender impossible? Not at all! By rooting out self-centeredness in thought, word and deed we can remove the focus from the limited ego-self, placing it instead on the eternally free God-Self.

Once we open our hearts to God, He will assist every step of the way. His loving presence puts worldly success in its proper perspective. We begin to see the needs of others; we can enjoy people, places and things without fear of their passing. Otherwise, the more we have, the more burdened we become. Buddha said, "He who is attached will suffer much." If we loosen our grip a little each day, we'll begin to taste the eternal success of our spirits.

Many of us are obsessed with recognition and adulation. What folly! Entertainers, sports figures and politicians of days gone by who lived solely for fame—where are they now? Bodies dead and buried, souls wondering why they never took the time to find out who they *really* were! If each of them sought their inner light as vigorously as they sought the limelight, their success would be everlasting. Then, all their recognition and rewards would rightfully go to God, the animating power behind us all.

As the Golden Age dawns, more and more souls are seeking liberation. Much change is in store; we must fasten our seat belts and place our trust in God, who is all opulence, the wealth of all wealth, the jewel in the heart of each of us. Offer everything up to the Father and live each day in self-correction. If we obediently follow our hearts, we will find our true success in God as He finally leads us back home.

Serving God on the Job

IN THIS AGE, we are pursuing divinity in many ways—seminars, intensives, retreats and the like—looking for a glimpse of our true selves. While all these methods are helpful, serving as stepping stones to higher development, a common complaint is that any piece earned is lost when we leave the sheltered environment of spiritual study and return to our normal routines. The need to make a living brings us back to our often unfulfilling jobs; before long, we are as uptight as we were before leaving! A conscious shift must take place if we are to maintain the bliss, balance and expand awareness we find in our spiritual work.

To see our jobs as service to God helps bridge the gap between the spiritual realm and the "real world" we live in. The inner kingdom we visit to release the anxieties of the "real world" is the everlasting *real world* of God. In contrast, the world of senses fades when we leave it at death. As we empower the inner world of spirit, the outer world must reflect the change in us, thus giving meaning to our day-to-day existence.

Our jobs don't have to be so stressful we awaken in shock, nor should they be so boring that we *never* wake up! Once we surrender our work to God, the subtle activity of the Divine pervades all we do. As we quiet the restless lower mind and enjoy spiritual peace, we can objectively witness the activities of the workday rather than react emotionally to them.

When confronted by someone in the workplace, we should look past their harsh manner and silently appeal to their God-Self. Even the most obnoxious, aggressive soul can be quieted by the power of the spirit if we begin to use our feeling natures rather than lashing out in anger and judgement.

We spend so much time at work; it would be a shame if we couldn't bring the peace of our spiritual practice into this part of our lives. It takes discipline to change our jobs from a chore to a joy, but with God's help anything is possible.

Be A Victor, Not a Victim

IN TODAY'S HARD TIMES, it is so easy to play the victim, to be crushed under the weight of life's problems. Seemingly the most natural motto to live by is, "Woe is me." If only we would realize that all our experiences—especially those that present the greatest challenges—help us rise above our limitations. Tough times can be our best teachers, strengthening instead of defeating us. If our lives were always easy, and we always knew what to expect, we would never grow. We resist change, yet change is our only certainty! How can we learn to be victorious in the face of life's adversities?

If we trust and have faith in our Eternal Father, we can be at peace no matter what we are going through. What others think of us is unimportant; it is what we think of ourselves that matters. Most people judge and criticize without having learned love and respect; their opinions change like the wind. Only when fault-finding ceases will peace and understanding rule our hearts and minds.

We must realize God truly loves us—through His love we gain strength and "self"-reliance. When we doubt ourselves, we doubt Him, for we are a part of Him. The vastness of the universe illustrates God's omnipotence; surely the same Force that cares for the universe will care for each of us as well. All God asks in return is our love and devotion to Him in all we do.

In order to better understand what happens when we lose our sense of peace, we can think of the mind as a glass, the emotions as water filling the glass, and our thoughts as sediment on the bottom. When the glass is shaken, the water stirs, causing the sediment to rise up and cloud the water. Similarly, when the mind is agitated through adversity, the emotions become unsettled, sending random thoughts racing through the mind and clouding it. There is no hope of achieving peace or understanding while the mind is in this state; by breathing deeply and centering ourselves in meditation, we can still our minds, calm our emotions and quiet our thoughts. The glass stops shaking, the water no longer swirls and the sediment settles back to the bottom, leaving a clear glass of water—a peaceful mind.

Be still and know that you are God. In this God-space, all problems vanish; they remain only if we choose to dwell on them. Remember, change those things you can and accept those you cannot. If we could take the energy we use to dwell on our difficulties and use it to dwell on God instead, we'd be much better off!

Our Father-Mother God, the Master Architect of our lives, always works in our best interests. The earth is not our permanent home; we are free spirits living temporarily in our earthly shells, like airplanes in their hangars preparing to fly back to a common point of origin. If we let our spirits take flight, no adversity can hold us back—we will achieve our final victory.

To Gain the World and Lose Your Soul

EVERYONE WANTS TO BE SUCCESSFUL in what he or she does in life. To excel at one's craft is a measure of success. As a society we admire excellence in sports, theater, government and in all walks of life, and we strive to be noticed and recognized by our peers. But can success of a temporary nature really be the only success we can experience? Aren't we limiting ourselves by sacrificing everything for a few fleeting moments in the limelight? I don't suggest that people should refrain from making something of themselves, but that they not be satisfied with the level of success alone.

God wants His children to taste the prosperity and opulence of His world, but also to acknowledge that it is *His* world. We are programmed by our parents and our peers to strive for the proverbial brass ring, to accumulate all we can and thus ensure our security. Yet this is only one of many other worlds Jesus referred to when He spoke of the collective House of God having "many mansions". It is our birthright not only to learn the lessons of this world, but to graduate into one of these other worlds, these higher expressions of self—where everything becomes God-oriented, not materially oriented.

It is only our misperception that makes God seem far from us. We should begin to thank the Father for all He has given us and open ourselves further to Him each day. All

God asks is that we love him and seek Him within the silence of our beings. This turning inward with love is the means by which we can most quickly achieve freedom and liberation. For five minutes each day, we should give our total attention to talking and listening in God-communion. Watch how this time, consistently spent, will bear abundant fruit, helping us gain the wealth of the spirit as the ways of our Creator are learned. To have outer wealth and yet be empty inside is true poverty; to have a heart overflowing with the love of God and our fellow man, regardless of worldly riches, is to be the wealthiest man or woman on earth. Many saints and holy men or women appear eccentric to worldly minded people since their outer lives seem strange or exceedingly austere, but the inner level of awareness these souls have achieved makes any worldly attainment pale by comparison. There is no higher opiate in life than the experience of God; that experience brings an ecstasy and joy nothing else can give. The only safe and liberating addiction is the longing for God-realization. This liberation, however, starts with baby steps, which in turn lead to large strides. As schoolchildren, we were often told to pay attention; we must again pay attention to our teacher, the I AM Presence, so we may graduate our earth schoolroom with high honors. These honors, my friends, will never fade.

Laughter, the Greatest Therapy of All

THE ROAD TO SELF-REALIZATION can be a joyous one, for spirituality is part of our natural state. While discipline is needed to conquer the flesh, unnecessarily harsh austerities only ensure a quick exit from the spiritual path. Renunciation can never be self-imposed, but must be a natural outgrowth of our own God-Selves. Once the seed of spirituality is planted deep within, daily watering and fertilizing is required for its growth. Just as the most successful gardeners love their gardens, when we love to meditate, to pray, to read, to prune our faults—then our inner gardens blossom quickly and steadily.

If we are to produce a beautiful spiritual bouquet, we can't take ourselves too seriously. The ability to laugh is one of our greatest gifts; it enables us to purge our souls of much darkness. Laughter can completely change the atmosphere around us where moments before we may have been overcome by a weighty problem.

Life is what we make of it; it can be a divine comedy or a divine tragedy. I am not suggesting we laugh in the face of all circumstances, for to do so would be foolish. Instead, we should cultivate a sense of humor regarding the play of life and our roles in it; this will help us forgive ourselves and others more quickly.

It is so important to release our dogmatic attachments and overcome the negativity life's problems can bring. Upon reflection, it's likely we'd find we can barely remember today what we would've fought over and died for ten years ago! Difficult situations and passionate beliefs come and go like the wind, but the truth of our perfection in God is everlasting.

Life shows us our many faces; it's up to us to decide which one fits, for we are simultaneously all, none and more than all of them. We are multi-dimensional beings, co-existing in many worlds; as we lose our fear of the unknown, it becomes easier to step into and out of these worlds until it is like stepping through a doorway. Jesus referred to the mobile spiritual body that makes these journeys as the *seamless garment of light*, or *Overself*. Within this Overself, we discover our true essence.

The Pharisees of old crucified Jesus because He lived the truth in every moment. He tried to show them how to let go of dogma and experience the fullness of their spirits, but they felt threatened by this Cosmic Being of great light; too seriously bound to their false egos, they couldn't relinquish their limited sense of power long enough to open freedom's door. Modern-day Pharisees exist throughout our world; hopefully their souls will surrender at this time, for Jesus will return as a Lion, not as a sacrificial Lamb.

For the sake of our souls and for the good of all mankind, we must learn to laugh at our frail egos and their self-created delusions. It is our birthright to experience a Christed body of light, but we must empty ourselves before we can be filled with this light. The world may seem like one big tug-of-war right now, but stay happy—the appointed time of our graduation into higher life is coming.

The Lesson of the Butterfly

It was a seemingly ordinary Long Island summer day; overcast sky, light breeze and uncomfortably high humidity. I was with my nine year old son John and infant daughter Sara, and we decided to go to a nearby park. The park was very small and simple in design; the perimeter was lined with houses, a common feature in this part of God's country. As Johnny helped me push Sara along in the stroller, we followed the path into the park.

First, we passed through an open, central section where we would later toss the incredibly aerodynamic discs that have replaced the Frisbees of my childhood. We continued through the park, enjoying the day and each other, talking and having the fun families naturally have. We decided to sit in a grassy area by a narrow wall no more than a foot high.

As we sat, we noticed a small butterfly serenely perched on top of the wall. We studied this butterfly, marvelling that it was not unnerved by our presence. With great curiosity and wonder we drew closer to our new-found friend. Johnny and I began to place our fingers near the butterfly; Sara cooed as one-year olds do. We took turns first touching, then gently stroking its wings. Our friend seemed to enjoy the contact, and we were transfixed by its openness and lack of fear. Next, we decided to see if it would perch on our fingers; of course, the butterfly obliged, reminding me of my pet parakeets of years ago and helping me silently say "hello" to my long-departed feathered friends.

In the midst of our enjoyment, another butterfly flew above us, causing ours to fly after it in defense of its territory. We hoped it would return, and were startled to feel it taking turns landing on my head, Johnny's head and my shoulder for intervals of twenty to thirty seconds or longer each time. The butterfly then perched on the edge of Sara's stroller; she decided to touch it, but with my baby's lack of dexterity, she would've lovingly squashed it. Johnny and I laughed, for the butterfly knew it was time to take off and did!

How well the butterfly symbolizes the grace, beauty and spontaneity of God and His creation. It also serves as a symbol of our liberation; as the caterpillar grows into a butterfly, so we each undergo a metamorphosis, evolving from human to divine.

As it came time to leave the park, I felt such deep thankfulness to our Creator for joining us in the form of our new friend, the butterfly. This unexpected encounter had held us spellbound for forty-five minutes or so, and I knew there were many lessons to be learned from it—that life unfolds in its own time, that we must simply remain alert and be patient until the messages we seek become clear, and that magic is occurring *now* all around us. We must serenely live in the moment as best we can, always keeping our eyes on the butterfly, a true symbol of freedom.

Change:
A Necessity for Growth

THE ONLY CONSTANT WE FIND in our lives is change. Every thing around us is in flux; to remain at peace, we must focus on the only constant part of our beings, the God-Presence within. As we anchor ourselves to this Magic Presence, we learn to flow with change rather than work against it, establishing an unshakable peace that truly does "pass all understanding". But how do we maintain this changeless God-like state amidst life's constant changes?

First, we must learn to embrace change; as we accept it, we being to find comfort where there was none, learning to be flexible through all of life's experiences. Since life reflects both our positive and negative sides, we must be willing to acknowledge our shortcomings as we see them and change accordingly. The quest for enlightenment has been compared to the peeling of an onion; our human natures are the many layers covering our souls at the center. Change hastens the peeling process! As we begin to see its benefits, we will no longer resist change but embrace it as a necessary part of our spiritual development.

Without change life becomes stagnant and uninteresting. The Old Testament states, "To everything there is a season and a purpose under heaven." Nothing happens by chance or by coincidence; in every experience there is a lesson to be learned and wisdom to be earned. To understand these lessons, it is essential to be poised and still inside; daily meditation and prayer is our spiritual food and must be ingested by our entire beings. In the repose we gain from these activities, we can understand our most difficult periods of change and move through them with ease.

Why the Earth Changes?

Recently there has been much talk of earth changes so cataclysmic as to result in a loss of two-thirds of the earth's population by roughly the year 2012; some say we may even see the end of the world. In order to understand this transition and be at peace with it, we must see the answer through our Higher or Divine Minds; then we will see these events as a necessary spiritual purification of the earth plane, not as the actions of a vengeful creator. As a being of the highest vibration and purest love, *God has not and never will forsake any of his Children*!

So why must Mother Earth purge herself? All the hatred, prejudice, greed, lust and other travesties occurring on her surface have altered her evolution as a living, breathing organism, poisoning our Earth Mother. Man has paved her shell, built overpopulated cities running on self-interest, polluted her waters for profit, depleted the ozone layer so he can no longer safely enjoy the summer sun, decimated her rain forests and built nuclear power plants that are no more than ticking time bombs. By creating a society based on greed and gratification and not on God, man has raped Mother Earth. Now, she must expel mankind's poisons and pollutants before she can again be the beautiful bio-satellite she was designed to be.

Our selfishness and corruption have brought this day of reckoning upon us. Rather than blaming God, or questioning His existence, shouldn't we try asking for His help instead? We must each look to ourselves and being to foster the most important relationship of our lives—our relationship with God.

We must establish as intimate a relationship with God as we can, for within this vast I AM or Christ Consciousness, there is *always* hope. None of the earth changes *must* happen, but if we look objectively at the world, the need for change is obvious. That is why we must change as a people; our efforts in the next ten to twelve years are *very* important! The Virgin Mother Mary has repeatedly urged us to pray and fast with regularity; these practices would help us to open to the Light and build a positive momentum of spiritual growth, thus lessening the intensity of or possibly averting many of the earth changes.

We must pull together as a great force! The energy and power of love-vibration must beam from each of us in order to counteract the forces of darkness. Be persistent and unshakable in this vision, like the Knights of the Round Table in their quest for the Holy Grail. Each of us must defeat the voice of the Anti-Christ within, fearlessly facing whatever tests we must endure. To aid us in our quest, we should set up regular prayer and meditation groups with family and friends; we must make a goal of saving the earth by saving ourselves the most important part of our lives.

I have come into the world to emphatically demonstrate that our Father-Mother God does indeed exist! The materialists who read this will scoff at these words, calling them another doom-and-gloomer or weird imaginings of another mad prophet; in their pride and ignorance, they don't want to change. Remember, they called Jesus a madman, a revolutionary, a blasphemer, a deluded soul. But those in Jesus' time knew the truth, as we now know it.

I have come to prepare the way for my brother Jesus as I did two thousand years ago; I have come to gather those who love God and our dear Earth Mother. We must open our minds and hearts and prepare a tabernacle within, for the hour is drawing close at hand. We must spread the word to all those we love out of love and not fear. This is the Omega, the end of times, with the new beginning to follow; there is no death, only a shift in consciousness. To each of you I say: Stay close to your light and be brave, strong and true to your soul, for God will never abandon you. As Jesus said, *"I AM with you always, even unto the end of time."*

    We are the children of the light; our Light, the Light of God in this world, cannot fail and will only grow stronger if we band together in true brotherhood and sisterhood, no only in word but in deed. We must each imbibe and act from the teachings of the Great I AM, leading to those around us as we are being led by the Father-Mother God within. Don't resist the earth changes; they must come, but what forms they will take depend on our efforts *now*. May our faith in God become so strong that nothing can shake our love for Him or for each other. Amen.

Non-Doership

"Without going outside, you may know the whole world.
Without looking through the window, you may see the ways of heaven.
The farther you go, the less you know.

Thus the sage knows without traveling;
He sees without looking;
He works without doing."

—From Aphorism #47,
Tao Te Ching, Lao Tse

THE SPIRIT WITHIN KNOWS ALL, sees all, does all; the ego perceives itself to be the doer and therefore remains bound. How difficult it is for the ego to respond similarly to victory and defeat, honor and insult, praise and blame.

"The power behind every activity of nature and of man is the power of God. To realize this truth is to be immortal."

—From the "Kena Upanishad"

Many of us have had the experience of non-doership—the feeling of being somehow removed from ourselves while performing a task, almost as if someone was lifting the burden from our shoulders. That "someone else" lightening our load at that time was God; however, *anytime* we want to release the sense of doership and taste the liberation of the spirit, all we need to do is ask God's help. Then, by witnessing the activity of life around us, observing ourselves in action and offering up the fruits of our actions to the Father, we can truly "let go and let God". The more we let go, the more freedom we attain; leaving our egos behind, we can taste the everlasting ambrosia of our souls.

I experienced non-doership for the first time the night that I was to sing a devotional song by Meher Baba many years ago. After going through the many nuances and faces of my ego prior to that evening, the moments just before we sang were very tranquil and amazingly serene. As the song was being performed, a glorious energy never experienced before took over me and my fellows in our singing group. As I was the "lead" singer of our spiritual quartet, the profundity of the experience increased the more we got into the song. I literally felt like I was standing behind myself observing myself as the song was being sung by me, but in a way that the me in "me" was no longer the "little me" that was driving me crazy only a few hours earlier.

As I felt waves and waves of such a pure and exquisite bliss, tears came from my eyes as I watched this new-found energy "perform" the chant better than ever before. The words on the music sheet moved in a rhythmic pattern letting me know emphatically that God was the doer. He was taking me along for my first of many glorious soul excursions. I often remember this first encounter with non-doership when my ego tries to grab hold and leave its indelible limiting stamp. The great Indian Saint Sri-Ramakrishna used the analogy of a woman straightening her hair every morning with that of reminding oneself that it is the God power who performs all actions and not the limited ego-self. And as such we must remain vigilant to stay free of the snares of the ego self. For the one morning that the woman forgot to straighten her hair, lo and behold, her hair was all kinky and tied in knots. In the same way, when we forget and allow our small ego to delude us into taking credit or discredit, our spiritual hair becomes all knotted up.

Whatever path you are on, tread it with joy and diligence. Do your disciplines and one day you no doubt will experience the ambrosia of non-doership. There is such great joy and liberation in surrendering to God's will and letting it be done in you. And once you are moved by the Great-I Am, your life will never be the same.

Honor Thy Mother and Father

When we were in spirit form, we choose our earthly mothers and fathers, hoping they would care for us and help us grow in body, mind and soul. But as we live our lives, our relationships with our parents often swing from harmony to chaos and back. It saddens me to see children at odds with their parents. We all have our reasons and we feel strongly about them, but maybe we should step back and look at what we do to each other. If we did, I think we would find there is no argument or misunderstanding that cannot be resolved through God's love.

We children must give love a chance in our relationships with our parents. Most parents have done the best they could with us; let's walk a few miles in their shoes instead of being so quick to judge them. Life can be very trying, and we are all prone to error; if God the Father was not eternally loving and judged our every mistake, no one would enter the kingdom of heaven!

Mothers and fathers share a unique bond with their children. My mother has always shown me her unconditional love. She watched as I became more and more involved in my quest for enlightenment. When friends dropped by and the conversation turned to spirituality, she usually went to the other room and turned on the television! Although she hasn't understood all that I have said or done, her love and support have always been there, and these I will cherish.

Overlook your petty differences—earthly life is too short to stand on ceremony. If your parents are still alive, express your love for them *now*; you need to say it and they need to hear it. Do something while it still counts! You'll be surprised to discover how your parents felt when you couldn't see past your own feelings.

We all want to love and be loved. Once we take the first step, there is no turning back. Let us neutralize the poisons of parent-child relationships gone wrong, and in so doing help heal the whole world.

Teach Your Children Well

Our children will be the caretakers of the world to come, so we must teach them well. We must help and encourage them not only to do well in school, obtain a diploma from a fine college and land a job with a good company; we must also assist in the awakening of their souls.

It is important for us to set aside our burdens and truly *listen* to our children. Listening to them is the first step in guiding their interests and talents toward their higher potentials in God. The younger the child, the more open he or she is, and the more readily that child will conform to any mold or pattern we set. However, children are innately spiritual. There is no need to force them into anything; we just need to remind them of the godly natures from time to time. As we work on ourselves and are clear in our own perceptions, we can give our children a strong spiritual foundation and still let them be children.

As parents, our hardest task is to let go of our children. They are only with us for a short time, so it is important to instill independence and strength in them as soon as they can begin to assimilate these characteristics. All things are attainable for our children, if we help keep the doorways to their souls open. We should not pressure them to be spiritual, but naturally allow them to discover their higher selves as they discover all other aspects of life. Most young souls today are alert to and aware of the coming earth changes, and they want to fulfill their roles. In fact, children are the parents of their parents in may cases; young people possess spiritual wisdom belying their years. An awakened parent will listen to and closely observe his or her children, realizing much can be learned from them.

Our children are the torch-bearers of the future; their souls chose their earthly roles before their embodiment on this plane. We must let our children know we love them unconditionally regardless of the mistakes they might make, for love is the golden key that unlocks all doors between ourselves and our children.

Sports Fans—Root For God

IT IS AMAZING TO FEEL the electricity of a crowd as they watch their home team at a football or baseball game. It is truly incredible when countless souls put their political, spiritual, sexual and ethnic differences aside and unite for the afternoon or evening. If the home team wins, everyone shares in the ecstasy. People are friendly and courteous as they leave the stadium; everyone is in a good mood. If the team loses, its fans are still united since they share in the disappointment. Some become upset and immediately vent their frustrations, while others stew quietly—perhaps for days.

It may seem silly to react so strongly to a sporting event, especially in light of its relative insignificance of our lives. When I was a boy, I remember going to church and praying for the New York Giants to win their games. My dad and I would watch each game as if our very salvations depended on the outcome. If anyone dared walk in front of the TV, they knew to walk quickly so we wouldn't miss a play! As I matured and grew in my spirituality, I began to wonder how different the world might be if we would root for God like we do for our teams.

God is not the remote, abstract energy that we make Him out to be. He is the energy that we are. I would love to be part of a gathering of 60,000 people where we are all singing our hearts our in praise and gratitude for all the Father has given us! If we took time to unite in God, in the celebration of His joy, can you imagine the loving and healing energies that would be spread among those there in the stadium? Can you visualize it pouring out over the whole planet and into the universe? I hope and pray a gathering of God's children does take place, where people can freely express their spiritual feelings. Evangelists can draw large crowds, but unfortunately the gospel of negativity they often preach paralyzes their audiences with guilt and fear. Yes, we must repent, but we must also see ourselves as sons and daughters of God who need direction, not as sinners who will go to hell if we don't change our ways; this hell-fire and brimstone charade only creates more confusion.

God is *love*; God is not fear, guilt or any other negative emotion we falsely attach to spirituality. Love God as you would your mother, father or best friend, and watch your imperfection fall away. Replace your negative stance with a positive one—gather together to sing and dance, then direct the ecstasy you feel to the Father who gives and gives, waiting patiently for His children to come home.

The Gift of Life

LIFE IS A PRECIOUS GIFT from our Heavenly Father. But when do we take the time to truly thank Him for all we've been given? Many of us expend so much energy pursuing a life of luxury, yet never thank God for what we acquire. And so we seem shallow and loveless, caring only about finding the path to material gain. This road, however, leads to death and destruction, for none of us were designed for the sole purpose of seeking to exceed the wealth of our fellow human beings.

Because our surface minds capture our whole attention so skillfully, many of us never stop to think what life or true success really is. The essence of life or success is found in the God-Self, the Oversoul or Christ-Consciousness, yet this Magic Presence sleeps in many of us. If we awakened our Higher Selves, we would experience peace and joy that nothing on earth could give. Materialism makes us selfish, judgmental and unstable, forever enslaving us to our own creations. One day the soul that clings to worldly goods will painfully exit the earth plane, vainly clutching his or her possessions. God wants His children to be happy and prosperous, but first He wants us to acknowledge our debt to Him for all He has given.

In this time of change, we must start to give back what God has given us lifetime after lifetime. "Kindness, Courtesy and Love" should be our motto in daily interactions. We mustn't only consider relatives and friends as family, for we are *all* brothers and sisters—one family, one energy, one love in God. Let's break down the walls dividing us and appreciate life by appreciating others.

Here is a simple exercise: Focus on the love in your heart as best you can throughout each day. As situations distract you, picture your love growing stronger. At each day's end, reflect on what transpired; write your thoughts in a diary if you like. Through daily practice, you will see the circumstances that bring out the worst in you; note your shortcomings and begin to immerse them in love. Don't condemn yourself when you digress, but intensify your focus. Soon love will flow constantly and effortlessly from your heart.

Everything we believe we possess belongs to God; only be daily surrender and renunciation can we grow in strength and attune to the Still Small Voice within. As one family under the Father, we must begin to appreciate His gifts to us—the birds, flowers, sky, trees, mountains, each other—and say "thank you". By opening our hearts in solemn thankfulness for God's world and the people in it, we will transform its atmosphere from darkness to light forever.

"Truth doesn't necessarily make friends but it does influence people."

Part IV

Heart
(Seat of Consciousness)

The Warrior's Heart

THE WARRIOR'S HEART IS FULL OF LOVE! The warrior's heart does not make war! But the warrior must take his stand to defend the Light and uphold the truth of humankind.

As the world around us begins to shed the old order to make way for the New Jerusalem we cannot be passive. We must all take up the sword of light with authority, knowing that our authority comes from on high. We are the brotherhood and the sisterhood of Light on this planet and we must all *act*.

If you are prompted from within to give a talk, work in a soup kitchen, write a book, or simply give your love wherever you go, then do that. Your Christ self, your overself, is giving you a gentle nudge forward, to be a helping hand and to inspire others in this time of great change.

We have always been taught to *dare*, to *do*, and to *be silent*. But now we must all act and gather those who are open to the new beginning.

Jesus sees a lot of talk around the planet, yet little action. He said we don't realize the supreme importance of our contribution to the *Great Work*. We are needed to create a window of consciousness in this world that will signal the re-entry of Jesus and the Ascended Host into matter.

To play our parts, we must activate the warrior's heart in ourselves and in our brethren. Do not be afraid to speak out or to make waves. In the long run you will doing your brothers and sisters a favor. The Ascended Host is helping all of us adjust to the coming changes. In turn, we are duty-bound to play our part.

Open your heart to Love. Open your mind to Truth. Help open the ears of our brethren to hear the trumpet call to Life.

The Glory of Love

"I am a man who will for fight for your honor,
I'll be the hero you're dreaming of.
We'll live forever knowing together
That we did it all for the Glory of Love."

"The Glory of Love", by Peter Cetera

THE GLORY OF LOVE is what service to God and mankind is all about. And the Glory of Love is about the incoming New Golden Age, the time when our creator's true love for His creation will raise us into a new frequency, a higher octave of light.

What a glorious time to be incarnate! Let us surrender our doubts, give up our resistances and put away feeling unworthy of fulfulling our collective destiny. Let us trust and accept the creator's divine blueprint. May we also now remember that we chose to serve the Father at this time in this place.

As you choose to be chosen you will find that your life will become the very manifestation of the Quickening. For when you sincerely open your heart to your creator, rapid changes will occur. But as you feel your heart become fuller, as the right action becomes clearer, and as your earthly burden seems to dissolve before your very eyes, remember the purpose of it all: the Glory of Love.

Therefore, dedicate your whole being to the Great Work. Put aside thoughts of self. Never mind the past and don't concern yourself with the far future. Concentrate your energy fully on the present moment. Intensify the desire to work for the common cause and ask to be strengthened for the tasks ahead.

Each breath you take is a chemical offering to God, so breath with great ardor and adoration for the Lord of the Universe. Jesus and the Ascended Host have stressed that we must all live each moment with greater and fuller awareness. And awareness, simply defined, is Love. Love for God. Love for each other. Love for Mother Earth. Love for ourselves. The more we love ourselves, the more we can help others.

There is so much mistrust and confusion in the world that we must become very secure within ourselves. We must know what is real and what is not. Think of the great credo: "Neither praise nor blame." Just observe both and realize they are illusions. When you endeavor to serve, remember that it is not for yourself that you act. It is for God, for the Glory of Love. True service is self-less giving.

And that, after all, is how Jesus was able to bless those who were suspicious of him, those who doubted, and even those who accused him. Jesus did everything for his Father and for the Glory of Love.

It is said that he or she who carries the flame of God shall live in a field of Glory. Do not be dismayed if you encounter resistance to the truth you know in your heart of hearts. Glory is found on the inner planes and is truly the Glory of Love Everlasting.

Conviction of the Heart

"Where are the dreams we once had?
This is the time to bring them back.
What were the promises caught on the tips
 of our tongues?
Do we forget or forgive?
There's a whole other life waiting to be lived when
One day we're brave enough to talk with
Conviction of the Heart."

"Leap of Faith", by Kenny Loggins

THE TIME HAS COME to speak the truth aloud, and to express outwardly what we know in our heart of hearts. For too long we have subjected our souls to the false powers of fear and doubt. For too long we have compromised the truth to avoid making waves.

Now we must lift ourselves out of indifference and insensitivity. We must replace darkness and pain with divine light and forgiveness. We must surrender our self-importance and speak from love in our hearts. For the heart is the home of the fearless hero that dwells inside us. The source of true power and authority. Deep inside the heart God makes His quiet presence known. It is up to each of us to find this voice and amplify it so that God can speak through us.

We must stand up now and boldly express the convictions of our hearts. It is up to us to trigger a profound change in the hearts and minds of our brothers and sisters. Our goal is to help all the individuals of this world regain their divine consciousness.

No longer can the tide of peace and love that is coming to the planet be held back. Those who are open to it are feeling a tremendous change in their consciousness as life manifests in an ever more accelerated fashion. But it is not enough to sit back content with the bliss of spiritualization. We must actively participate in the rebirth of the Earth. We must cast the density of the human coil and speak the truth. Truth is simply letting love guide your every thought, word, and action. Living the truth is simply letting God work through you. Be humbly great in God!

> "And down your streets I've walked alone,
> As if my feet were not my own.
> Such is the path I chose.
> Doors I have opened and closed.
> I'm tired of living this lie;
> Fooling myself—Believing we're right
> When I've never given love with any
> Conviction of the Heart."
>
> "Leap of Faith", by Kenny Loggins

Are you tired of living the lie of illusion? Do you want to eradicate fear and negativity? Speak the truth from your heart. Rise above the trepidation and the justification of the ego.

Love is the glue that holds all of creation together. Love creates everything—planets, people, galaxies, universes. Love is what God continuously pours out upon us. We have been made in His image.

Each of us must surrender to true Love so that we can collectively destroy the illusion of pain and suffering that now controls the planet. The time is upon us to bring about the New Jerusalem, to fulfill our mission and establish the consciousness of unity upon the Earth.

To feel that higher frequency or vibration is to let go of thought and to allow the mind and heart to become one. All one needs to do is to still one's self in prayer and meditation. Then it is possible to communicate and be communicated to.

> "It's been too many years of taking now.
> Isn't it time to stop somehow?
> Air that's too angry to breathe;
> Water our children can't drink.
> You've heard it hundreds of times;
> You say you're aware,
> Believe, and you care, but
> Do you care enough?
> Where's your Conviction of the Heart?"
>
> "Leap of Faith", by Kenny Loggins

Do we care enough to act? Do we dare to drop all psychological separations, all the ethnic, racial and nationalistic identifications, in order to make a difference? I implore you to search for your conviction of the heart. Stand up, take your stand, and rid yourself of fear and apathy. Help create the change we all need. The convictions of all our hearts are needed now to bring about the New Jerusalem.

> "One with the earth—with the sky.
> One with everything in Life.
> I believe we'll survive if we only try.
> How long must we all wait to change
> This world bound in chains that we live in;
> To know what is to forgive and be forgiven."
>
> "Leap of Faith", by Kenny Loggins

Love and Unity

LOVE IS THE MOST POWERFUL FORCE in the universe, connecting us all like beads on God's great rosary; to master love is to master life. All paths, all disciplines lead to the simplicity of the heart and its vast capacity to love.

We should take time each day to explore our heart centers. Placing our hands over our hearts, we can leave the conscious mind behind for a few minutes; we begin to *feel* life rather than analyze or judge it. The heart acts as an internal barometer, balancing our thinking and feeling natures. A shift takes place within as selfishness, anxiety, doubt and fear begin to fade. As we empty ourselves of the falseness of ego, we manifest the fullness of spirit.

We all want to love and be loved, but most of us are mired in ego-driven fears and defenses. Love is found by dropping our defenses and releasing our fears. Not to be holding onto them! Instead of dealing with our own problems, we often escape into dependent relationships with other people, with work, with dangerous substances—but our inner needs are never met. The emptiness we feel can only be filled when we *completely* surrender to the love of God in our hearts. When we make this commitment, the stairway to the eternal rises before us. At times, this path seems steep and lonely; but instead of losing faith in God, we should focus on the heart, the seat of consciousness where our supply of love is replenished. This Divine Love within can be an inexhaustible source of ecstasy, lifting our spirits as much as we allow.

Love and Unity

We must hold fast to kindness and compassion even when the world seems lost in darkness. The outer world is an illusion seeking to mask the Divine Self within. When we can love the Lord our God with all our hearts, souls and strength, and love our neighbors as ourselves, the mysteries of life will be revealed to us.

Regardless of the mistakes we have made, God *never* judges us. The Father is a being of love, intelligence and majesty, with a limitless capacity for forgiveness. Just as He forgives us, we must forgive ourselves and others, especially our enemies. Each has a lesson for us if we can objectively *see* it.

As we cleanse ourselves of resentment and bitterness and radiate love and forgiveness, we clearly see the equality of all God's creatures. Remember, united we stand and divided we will surely fall; we are truly, deeply, intimately *one*. We should silently say "not two" as we encounter each other. This affirmation will begin to break down the walls that separate us.

We are in the Omega, the end of time, with the new beginning to come. Our duty as Children of the Light is to purify ourselves and surrender to love. If we want to effect change, we must start with ourselves. Then our example will spread to all corners of creation. Drink from God's fountain of eternal life, nurture love every day, and bring ye the heavens onto the earth.

We Are One Family in God

Close family relationships are important to most of us. Because of the degree of intimacy involved, they can also be the most troublesome. Family members can get on our nerves and push our buttons like no one else; it seems familiarity really does breed contempt!

All relationships begin with our relationship to ourselves. If we are happily aligned with our Higher Selves, all our relationships, not only those with our immediate families, will benefit. As we contact our true essences, the Christ Consciousness within, we start to see Him in everyone and everything. Thus, the notion of the world as "one family" becomes a reality, not just a nice idea.

This feeling of unity comes from our love of God. As Jesus said, "Love one another as I have loved you." When our hearts are open, we express God's spirit; our capacities to feel and to love increase. This more fully realized love remains strong through both positive and negative experiences. We are masters of our own destinies and *love is the golden key* to our mastery. Turning this key, we open an inner door that leads to God. As we identify this same God in each other, we see His face in every face.

Membership in the family of man helps each of us return to our roots. Spiritual teachings throughout the ages have been founded on love and respect; unfortunately many of us try to rely on our own knowledge rather than on the sacred knowledge of the universe. (Sun Bear, a Native American spokesperson, has described contemporary men and women as having large heads, stick-like bodies and tiny little hearts!) We must all recall our roots in love, harmony and fellowship; then we can God-consciously care for the earth, as well as for each other.

Living as one family under the Father, we learn that we gain by giving and lose by taking. Giving roots out selfishness and kills the Anti-Christ, our greatest enemy. When our hearts become as full as our minds, we will live naturally and effortlessly as the family of man.

By controlling the ego we can begin to heal our unhealthy relationships, even those with our immediate families. We must acknowledge the Christ power as the animating force behind our lives. As we generate peace, love and understanding, we will truly become one family and help move the earth toward its next level of expression.

America—The Torch-Bearer of the Light

THE UNITED STATES OF AMERICA has been chosen to carry the torch of spiritual light, setting the example for the rest of the world in the coming Golden Age. We live in a land that is rich in humanistic and spiritual tradition. Our founding fathers—men such as Washington, Franklin and Jefferson—directed America toward "liberty and justice for all" over two hundred years ago. Our early statesmen were more subtle in reference to God, yet symbols of spiritual freedom exist on our dollar bill—the all-seeing eye of the capstone atop the Great Pyramid and the phrase *E Pluribus Unum*, which is Latin for "one out of many", for example.

Over the course of our history, many great statesmen have lived and died for the freedom and equality of all Americans; our present-day leaders aspire to no less. Let's walk a mile in their shoes as they make decision after tough decision. These men and women, aware of the greater implications that lie before them and the people of this country, are doing the best they can; as fellow brothers and sisters, they need our love and support. Surely, we all feel the strain in this challenging time. Understanding and compassion for one another should be foremost in our hearts.

Yes, the United States is where the New Jer*USA*lem will emerge! The Return of the Dove will occur when Jesus and the Legion of 144,000 Ascended Masters return to this physical plane to gather righteous souls. They will also initiate the "quickening", moving the people of America and the rest of the world into a fifth-dimensional reality. We should envision this world-to-come in our mind's eye, giving love, support and positive affirmations at this time of great testing and challenge.

We must all join together in one great truth under God. It is time for spirit and science to become indivisible one; for all religions to see beyond their dogmatic interpretations of spiritual truth; and for people of all races, nationalities and political affiliations to set aside their differences. Though the world at present is hardly perfect, we should still appreciate it as it is. Our acceptance of God's great plan as it unfolds in the present can only help usher in the rapturous future we have all dreamed of.

We in the United States of America *can* bring in this Golden age of the New Jer*USA*lem, but first we must all surrender to the will of our Almighty Father-Mother God. This is a propitious time, a time to usher in the fullness of light and love so many of us desire, a time to make way for the New Jer*USA*lem that is most assuredly coming.

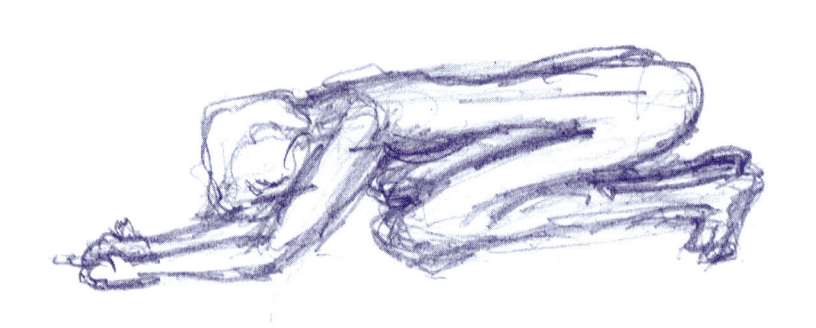

The Second Birth

"Through his luminous body, man believing in the existence of the true Light—the Light of this universe—becomes baptized or absorbed in the holy stream of the sound. The baptism is, so to speak, the second birth of man and is called Union with God through Love, without which man can never comprehend the real internal world, the Kingdom of God."

"Then we become the true Light, which lighteth every man that cometh into the world."

—John 1:9

"Verily, verily, I say unto thee,
Except a man be born again
He cannot see the Kingdom of God."

—John 3:3

How does one prepare for the second birth? Is it attainable while living in the world? Can one be a householder and still be born again? The answer is a resounding "Yes!" It does not matter what point you are at in your life. You can prepare for your second birth.

The only requirement is love; that love of God which is constantly drawing man toward the Kingdom of God. All spiritual disciplines aim at developing one's love of God. Little by little one can break the chains of the ego by fasting, praying, meditating, practicing silence and giving selfless service to others.

Pure devotion is the easiest and safest way to attain God Realization. Recognize devotion in its many forms and then expand on them, for they are essentially aspects of love of God.

The dedication of a scientist to a project that is beneficial to the whole is a form of pure devotion. The pure devotion of parents to their children is another. Yet another form of devotion is a publisher's desire to produce a message of hope for the upliftment and enlightenment of mankind.

In the East, the devotion of daily life is called "dharma", or duty. When the duty is performed with love it brings liberation and helps prepare us for the second birth.

As you expand this aspect of love, whether you sing in a church choir, chant in a meditation group, recite the Torah in a temple, or quietly sit and gaze into the infinite sky with an overflowing heart, you create the space inside yourself to be baptized or absorbed in the holy stream of the sound—the word—God.

Devotion to God is the simplest and surest way to go home. Do your work more intently. Do it with more love and the results will follow. Rather than looking for the fruits of your actions, aim at expanding and strengthening your love of God. That is the way to prepare yourself for the second birth.

I was shown via a powerful dream the impending "Second Birth" for the multitudes. On one shore was a fisherman casting out a very large "lure" and subsequently catching an enormous fish. Then my attention was drawn to hundreds of thousands of people on the opposite shore of the elliptically shaped lake, lined up following one another to the far end of the lake. As my attention followed the multitudes of people, if came upon an individual dressed all in white baptizing the people one by one, initiating them into their "Second Birth."

As more and more awaken to their true selves through their "Second Birth" the seed of the "New Jerusalem" can then take root in their consciousness, bringing about the world heretofore only hoped and dreamed about.

Joy, the Road to Freedom

As we embark on the spiritual journey, we often take our austerities too seriously. To overcome our earthly desires, we must be steadfast in our practices. But if we are new to the disciplines of our particular paths, or we have journeyed for awhile and our labors are not bearing fruit, something may be missing.

Remember what Bobby McFerrin sang—"Don't Worry, Be Happy." Meditation, fasting, scriptural and spiritual reading, chanting and spreading goodwill through our interactions with others are all forms of spiritual work, but they can only help us grow if we enjoy them. If we do this work as if we are taking castor oil, our progress will be slow and arduous. *Joy is truly our road to freedom*. All that we do in life must be done with our whole hearts; if we are half-hearted, we will only reap half the benefit. We don't have to change our teachers, our paths, what we read or when we meditate; we must simply change our attitudes! What we love to do, we do well because it helps us connect to spirit. *God is joy beyond mortal comprehension*; *God is bliss transcending all earthly delights*.

Saints and sages have always regarded God as the highest opiate known to man and have lived by this principle. To fully express our spirits is to experience an intoxication that makes our normal means of mood-alteration—alcohol, for example—seem inadequate. God wants His children to be happy, for joy makes the ascent to Him swift and painless. We feel pain only when judging the past, or when projecting into the future with uncertainty. Be in joy *now*; experience oneness with God *now*, for He is within us.

We may need to work in order to center our beings, but this work leads to a joy-filled, deeply rewarding existence. Walking the spiritual path empties us so we can be filled with the God-Presence. God is a treasure within us, waiting for us to rediscover Him. By remaining joyful even in the face of trials and adversity, we serenely pass all of life's tests.

God wants us to succeed in our struggles and come home to Him. (There's plenty of room in heaven, so don't worry about overcrowding!) We each have an eternal garment of light, or Overself, waiting to reunite with us. As we let go of the known world and embrace the life to come, our joy multiplies—we are forever free. There is nothing to fear; God will never let us be harmed. Thus we must continually strengthen our trust and faith in him until our belief becomes second nature.

We are all eagles of light and love, ready to soar through the universe—but first we must let go of the earth and its illusions. If we each follow our bliss and find those things that deeply satisfy us, we can enjoy our God-filled flights through life.

Seeing with Our Hearts, Not Our Minds

Jesus said, *"Unless you be like a little child, you shall not enter the kingdom of heaven."* The eyes of a young child see love and only love. Children don't judge or criticize; they truly live in the moment. Those of us who have children should let *them* teach *us* well!

For adults and children alike, love characterizes the light, separating it from the darkness. We must each take inventory of those aspects of ourselves that prevent us from love more completely . Do we hold grudges? Do we lack forgiveness? Must we become arrogant and intolerant to build self-esteem and self-confidence at the expense of others? Do soured relationships from the past steal from the present? Do we love only family and close friends while mistrusting the rest of the world? Can we only relate to those in our intellectual and spiritual levels? Do we dislike certain ethnic or religious groups? Are we so caught up in materialism that we don't stop to enjoy life?

It is a rare person who can answer "no" to all these questions. We must be honest with ourselves and begin to remove the darkness from our hearts. The heart reflects whatever we feel; why not feel joy, peace and the ecstasy of life? If we diligently work to open and cleanse our hearts, the universe will help us, for as we take ten steps toward God, He takes a thousand toward us.

As the fire within our hearts burns, we must keep feeding it bigger and bigger logs of non-love. The heat of our inner fire can burn away all impurities. This is why the American Indians have used sweat lodges and why we run high fevers when we go through an intense purge. Let the cosmic fire burn hot within us, burning away our hatred and fear!

If we looked at life through the eyes of a child, we'd see magic in our everyday existence. Instead, we let our lower minds steal the life-energy from us. There is no joy in feeling superior or inferior, smarter or less intelligent, over-confident or lacking in confidence. The lower mind, trapped by these pairs of opposites, hopelessly swings back and forth like a monkey swinging from limb to limb. We must break the bondage of our monkey-minds and attune to our hearts instead.

Just as we are hyper-conscious of money, paying close attention to salaries, savings and investments, we also need to keep track of our dearest investment—the love energy in our hearts—which pays dividends to all the world. With overflowing accounts of love, we can contribute eternally to one another in the light of our illumined hearts and souls.

The Healing Power of Music and Dance

One of the most enjoyable ways of contacting the God-presence within is through music. The earth is the planet of music and healing; song vibrates through our lives both internally and externally. Yet we must all ask ourselves, "Am I singing the song of liberation and love, or the song of death and destruction?"

Consider today's music, for example. The positive tone of some songs encourages us and gives a sense of well-being, but other limit rather than enlighten us by their negativity. We must use the powers of discrimination God has given us when choosing music for our listening enjoyment. (Rock and rap fans, take note: Studies have shown that loud, abrasive sounds retard plant growth. Plants are living organisms, and so are we!) Negative music is noise pollution—it frays our nerves and endangers our health. Positive music, however, helps us connect with deep feelings and with our spirits.

Chanting, or singing the name of God, can help to harmonize our lives. When people gather to express their love of God and life in song, the magic of their spirits emerges. The intoxication felt while chanting is the sweetest nectar of the God-presence. This expression of devotion is the quickest, easiest, most natural way to achieve God-communion.

The cleansing that occurs during chanting helps us experience vital feelings of clarity and wholeness. As the soul's vibration is raised through song, the entire being is uplifted: The chakras are cleansed, the nervous system is bathed in prana or life force, the mind is stilled and the heart expresses the fullness of its love. We are now free to be fully creative and open to fulfilling the roles God has planned for us. By singing the songs of the Father, we come much closer to our true selves.

Any singing helps free us of unnecessary tension. When we are in our cars and hear a positive song on the radio, we should sing along, feeling the vibrations of our voices. Doesn't that feel good? It should, because the healing power inherent in these vibrations is the reason we have been given voices. We were never meant to shout angry lyrics, but to express love and healing in song.

We can physically express our enjoyment of music through dance. Dancing energizes us; the exercise it offers helps purge negativity, which is why we dance at most birthday celebrations, wedding parties and other special occasions. Yet we must be careful to avoid dancing to music that satisfies the senses but kills the spirit. Choose wisely. Move beyond the sensual and dance the Godly dance.

The Sufis, or whirling dervishes, have long known the secrets of letting dance carry them into spiritual ecstasy. We can also dedicate our dancing to God, freely expressing ourselves in a physical sense. We mustn't hold back, for joy and happiness await once we let go of restraint and self-consciousness. Through dance, we can recapture the carefree feeling of childhood. As God's children, this is how we should live.

Singing, dancing and enjoying inspiring music can open us to the music of the spheres. It is our heritage to hear and move with these celestial sounds, to contact God through His song. "Universe" means "one song", the song of God that plays all around and within us. Let us sing and dance so that we may feel all the sweetness of His presence. In the gifts of music and movement, we have the means to set our souls free. If we use these gifts intelligently and lovingly, we will sing and dance with the Father for all eternity.

How to Pray Successfully

It can be very discouraging when we feel our prayers are not being heard. We think, "Oh, God has got the whole universe to run. I guess he doesn't have time for me." Applying these earthly concepts to Our Creator is simply ridiculous. The fault, if any, lies with us and not with God. If we want to be heard, we must pray persistently and consistently, knowing exactly what we want. Our prayers must be focused through the careful use of our powerful, energizing breath.

Prayer without breath-energy has no power. We must give everything we have to reap the benefits, getting on our hands and knees and humbling ourselves before the Lord of the universe. Only then an we make our requests heard. As we pray, we should visualize our prayer already answered and the result already actualized. This action helps to bring our needs into manifestation. If we are steady, faithful and intense in prayer, we won't be disappointed.

Of course, what we pray for is also extremely important. Most of us pray for better jobs, good relationships and material pleasures we think will make us happy. But this is a short list; we must expand our horizons to include the liberation of our limitless spirits. We can pray for our Overselves, our spiritual "doubles" consisting of all love, wisdom and peace, to contact us. As the Overself hears our call, it draws even closer until we unite with it.

Jesus' evolution brought Him into contact with His Overself. At first He said, "Of myself I can do nothing; it is all the will of the Father." As His prayer to His Overself intensified, He could then say, "I and the Father are *One*." When this occurs for us, all else fades away. This victory and the resulting happiness are ours forever.

We should shoot an arrow toward the stars, making our aim straight and true. Think of the body as the bow, the breath as the string across the bow, and the voice as the arrow. Our words of prayer, intensely directed straight at the Godhead, cannot fail to hit their target. Intense prayer is always heard, but we must be patient; time can truly be a test. As we reach for the knowledge, power and love of the universe, we must be totally free of ego before our hearts can be completely filled. We mustn't doubt the coming of this fulfillment. We may think we are ready now, but the Father-Mother God must be convinced of our worthiness before our victories are won. Pray—not only for personal gains, but for the coming of the day when the entire earth and her people will again align harmoniously with God.

Forgiveness

"Forgive us our trespasses, as we forgive those who trespass against us." So says the Lord's Prayer, and so should this be our credo in life. Even though we try to resist the temptations that are directed toward us each day, as human beings we sometimes make mistakes. How do we deal with this imperfect part of our humanness?

By watching young children we get an idea how to deal with life's difficulties. Children generally get over their heartaches quickly, while adults tend to hold onto hurts and disappointments—sometimes until death. Not only do we pollute our auras, the fields of energy surrounding our physical bodies, but we also contaminate the living being that is our planet. Thoughts and feelings travel into the atmosphere at a rapid rate and extend far into space. Humanity's discord is literally choking the planet, preventing its full expression of light. We need to understand that our good thoughts and feelings add to the light-nature of this planet, while our discord adds to the dark effluvia already surrounding it.

Forgiveness is the key; it is the *only* way to correct this condition. First, we must learn to forgive ourselves of our misdeeds. We must take full and unflinching responsibility for our lives; blaming others is nothing but a cop-out. We must start by seeing ourselves as children of God, sons and daughters of the Most High—gods and goddesses in embryo. We must not see ourselves as sinners, for that is erroneous and will only add to our ignorance. To transform in and through God is to become what we already are. Sounds too good to be true, doesn't it? It sounds too simple. But simple, humble souls are the ones that find God, not those filled with intellectual pride and hypocrisy. We should get down on our knees each day and let go of our faults and mistakes by asking the Father for forgiveness. God is a being of boundless love; He created His children and waits patiently for them to return to Him. We must open our hearts in forgiveness and allow the healing energy of the Christ-Consciousness to root out our deficiencies. We should never feel unworthy of this forgiveness, for our guilt has not place in God's kingdom.

As we learn to forgive ourselves by asking for God's forgiveness, we then can forgive others. Before we go to sleep each night, we should send out rays of forgiveness to the people that have hurt us the most, naming each of them. This action sets a positive energy field in motion, enabling those we name to forgive themselves. This energy, through the power of love, will return to us with accumulated force. It's a "win-win" situation; we win, our transgressors win, and best of all the planet wins, as it is able to breathe in more light.

We must constantly send out these positive vibrations, even if our adversaries do not soften their stances. Our light must be more tenacious than their darkness. If we always carry the torch of God and keep alive His Flame in our hearts, we open doors and walk down paths as yet unimaginable to us.

Repeat this after naming those whom you wish to forgive: *I Am the Violet Fire of Forgiveness and the Violet Transmuting Flame of All Inharmonious Action and Human Consciousness.* This will set the purifying flame of the "Violet Fire" into motion. It is also self-sustaining! Its job is to remove negativity and all discord. It is an aspect of the Violet Ray which is headed by the Great God Being, St. Germain. Use this ray and its consuming fire every night before you go to sleep. Also call out to St. Germain and other members of the Ascended Host.

St. Germain lived other lives as well. In one life he was Joseph, Jesus' father. Another was as Merlin the Magician of King Arthur's court. His last was as Sir Francis Bacon, called the "Wonderman of Europe." He won his spiritual victory and became known as St. Germain. His teachings via his messenger, Godfre Ray King, are called *The Unveiled Mysteries, The Magic Presence,* and *The I Am Discourses.* I highly recommend these works as they are very pure, centering, and liberating.

Use the Violet Fire inwardly and outwardly for your personal healing and that of *Earth Mother* as well. It is a very powerful tool used by the *Great White Brotherhood* in their mystery schools and retreats for thousands of years. Initiate and invoke your Divine right for the good of all. In time you will see it with your mind's eye. It is a beautiful sight to behold. If at first you don't see it, don't get discouraged. Once you set it in motion, it works whether you see it or not. So persist and be diligent with your purification removing your doubts and fears along the way. Use God's gift to us in the form of His *Violet Transmuting Fire* which will help you to play your part in this great play of life.

Giving Is Better Than Receiving

GIVING IS ONE OF THE KEYS to making spiritual progress while walking life's path. In this world we are often taught to acquire, to take, to conquer, to possess, to own. But it is only by letting go of ownership that we discover who we really are.

A life of serving and giving from the heart is the sure road to spiritual freedom. But how can we live this way in a world that seems so full of takers? How can we accomplish our spiritual ends without being taken advantage of?

As we learn to give without looking for something in return, little by little we begin to set the soul free. As long as materialism exists in this world, we must work for a living. The profit motive has enslaved men and women from the beginning of time; unfortunately, this restriction will continue until the material wheel no longer spins.

In everyday life, we can give ceaselessly in seemingly small ways. To smile, to let the other car into traffic while driving, to help an older person with his or her packages, to help a neighbor complete a chore without compensation gives one a good feeling, does it not? We always feel good when we lend a hand and someone says "thank you". We might not think these small occurrences mean much, but they send peace, goodwill and harmony into the atmosphere. These positive vibrations are especially needed now to stem the tide of darkness and ignorance flooding our world.

While we are giving in small ways, the larger ways will manifest as we show our Creator that our intent is pure and our only motive is to spread love. Giving becomes as natural as brushing our teeth once we become aware of the love within. We must all express this love and connect with one another. Joining together in this way would create a domino effect: As we are helped, so we help, and as we are shown courtesy, we give courtesy in return. We can all begin to form a closer union with others as we pursue our daily activities. Then as God asks us to make a deeper commitment to Him, we will be ready to hear His clarion call. There is nothing eternal on this plane of existence except for our ceaseless giving. All our achievements, adulation and material gain mean nothing in the face of the Divine. It is better for us to be recognized by the Father and ignored by all of mankind than to have everyone on our side. Always remember how Jesus stood alone amidst His accusers, maintaining His focus on the Father. You might think this stance could only have been taken by Jesus, the Son of Man, yet each of us can achieve this divine posture if we give everything to God.

Jesus said, "Empty yourself and you shall be filled with the Holy Spirit." We must give all we have to God and realize His desire is for us to live in brotherhood and peace. If we stop thinking only of ourselves, we gain a measure of control over the ego and allow our natural spirit to come forward. Giving, living and loving is our birthright. By acknowledging the needs of others, we can break the chains of discord around us and heal the planet in its hour of need.

The Role of Womankind in the Golden Age

WOMEN ARE THE FOUNDATION OF SOCIETY, just as they have been since the beginning of time. In this age, as consciousness evolves at an accelerated pace, we will all begin to realize the value and importance of the feminine principle. Women are the mothers of society, the tender hearts, the compassionate ones who in may instances have been the sole force holding their families together.

That women bear children should alert us to their special place in God's kingdom. But because many men have fallen into an egocentric, purely sensual existence, unaware of feminine divinity, women are often viewed in a totally different light. They are looked upon as sexual objects, taken advantage of in business matters and considered inferior by the chauvinistic male populace.

Many men seem to be reluctant to explore their higher consciousness. At many spiritual centers, there is a predominance of women. Why is this? Women seem to be more open to change; they are often willing to explore spiritual practices that many men would scorn because men tend to fear the emergence of their sensitive sides and the intuition, compassion and understanding such soul-searching would bring.

The emergence of the yin or feminine principle (which also exists in men, by the way!) is the key to the success or failure of the proposed "Golden Age". Women must give up their timidity, their conditioned acceptance of second-class status. This assertion of the feminine identity is beginning to be seen in the business world; still, women so often suppress their feminine strength and develop masculine weakness, feeling that adopting mens' ways is the best way to compete. It is on a day-to-day spiritual level that women must step forward and assert themselves. By exhibiting leadership and offering guidance to husbands and boyfriends and male acquaintances, women may help men become more complete. Then not only will men possess the strength, energy and focus needed to survive in this materialistic world, but they will also be able to express the kindness, tenderness and creativity of their feminine sides, becoming *real* men. Women must not be afraid to stand up to the men in their lives, though they may be larger in stature or louder in voice. Read between the lines of their irrational tirades; men are dying inside, trying to let their true selves out. *They need a woman's help*!

The harshness of life in the world we have created has cut so many of us off from our hearts, men and women alike. We increasingly attach to the material, not knowing how to let go. For those women who are awake know that the greatest expression of love is leading the men in your life upward by setting an example of action and not be lecturing. Words may only arouse their already overactive egos. Lead by example, and through their love for you they will change. We all *must* change, for the world is in a time of great crisis. Do your share by compassionately carrying the torch of Love wherever you go.

I had a very vivid dream some time back that signified the importance of "womankind" in the forthcoming "Golden Age." It took place by the seashore along the Atlantic Ocean. There was a whole legion or troop of women in battle fatigues with helmets being too large, uniforms not fitting properly and the "army" not looking too ready for any kind of battle. In the dream, I was in spirit, not body, going up and down the rows of God's feminine warriors straightening out their battle garb and inspiring them to be confident and not afraid of the "enemy" that was approaching. We were in the dunes looking over the ocean waiting for the moment of action. Toward the end of the dream, a few men showed up to offer their assistance. The dream ended with all of us looking out over the sea and our opponent never appearing.

This dream shows how important the Goddess is in the War of Love. Women have been held back by a patriarchal society far too long now. Your time for emergence has come! So stand up and make your presence felt to solidify and anchor the vibration of the feminine or "love vibration" on the emerging "new earth." This of course does not exclude "whole" or "real men" open to the feminine within and without. It simply signifies that things are about to become balanced and harmonized by the grace, beauty, compassion, love, and ecstasy of the "God/Goddess" within us all.

Adversity

ALL OF US FACE ADVERSITY at some time. We want life to be smooth and harmonious, so why are some of our experiences so difficult to endure? If God is truly loving, how can He expect us to cope in such trying situations?

Just as the Chinese symbol for crisis has as its counterpart the symbol for opportunity, so our lives continually present us with adverse situations that ultimately aid in our growth. Each trying circumstance can help us reach deeper inside ourselves and find the peace, wisdom and strength to light the way through the seeming darkness of human experience.

As the knowledge gained by facing adversity penetrates our heart of hearts, we begin to allow the Father's Will to be done. Our faith in Him will face many tests, but if we see these as necessary initiations into our Higher Selves, we will maintain our love for and trust in the Master Planner.

God does have our best interests at heart. We, in return, must give up every ego-based desire, possession and idea, whether sensual, materialistic or ideological. Only then are we empty enough to allow the fullness of God's Light inside. Instead of complaining during trying times, we should embrace them fully with a glad heart and be peaceful warriors filled with faith and trust in God. If we truly want freedom and liberation, we must accept all tests placed before us.

Jesus said, "Straight and narrow is the path, being as fine as a razor's edge." The higher we climb, the steeper our climb becomes, but the wisdom of God is such that we are presented with tests only when we can handle them. Each crisis is necessary in order to show us that the courage needed to rise above adversity exists in us all.

Yes, walking the spiritual path is like climbing a mountain; we must be as focused and persistent in our pursuit of God as a mountain goat, ever climbing higher in spite of temporary slips and slides. If we similarly face the obstacles that adversity presents us, nothing and no one can stop us from our goal of oneness with the Father.

God tests us and will shake our tree, so to speak, to bring out the desired fruit. As I expressed previously, the emotional adversity of losing a best friend and father in a short period of time caused me to make my turn back toward God. After I was well established on the path, he dropped another bomb in my lap.

He literally expressed his will causing my long-term marriage to dissolve. It was a difficult transition since I loved my family which included two children. I often refer to this period in my life as the "agony and the ecstasy." While this painful transition was going on, my past lives as "Elijah the prophet" and later as "John the Baptist" were revealed to me in many ways and forms. The emotional trauma I was going through caused me to doubt many of the messages and guidance I was receiving. I simply needed to be sure of this information before I could hold it in my heart as truth. And reveal it he did in such a surprising and beautiful manner that I was brought to tears.

God was teaching me many lessons. As he repeated to me often, *my son, you are gaining on the inner planes of worth and not losing* as your conscious self seems to think. God, in his/her infinitely loving way, was saying to me to just hang in there for there was a beautiful destiny in store if I could weather this storm. And stormy it was for I experienced every emotion imaginable. However, I learned a great deal from this adversity. I now trusted God like I had never done before. I also learned to be more completely detached since I had to leave the house I was living in. Early in my training, I read how spiritual teachers would have their students move from their homes or even build houses and then subsequently tear them down. This was all to teach them to detach from the physical, material plane. Little did I know I would be learning this lesson at this point of my life. Mysterious are the ways of God and the true spiritual teachers on the earth. Listen to us for we only have your higher interests at heart.

So realize that none of us are immune from the tests that ultimately strengthen us if we don't fold our tents and quit the path. Trust God when he is in fact moving you forward despite your earthly inclination to stay in a comfort zone of family and friends. When you say "yes" to God, be ready for the bumps and bruises of growth as you climb the spiralling stairway to Heaven.

The Leap of Faith

At the conclusion of *The Indiana Jones Trilogy*, Indiana has successfully passed his first two trials. Now he faces his ultimate test: The Leap of Faith. Indy must cross a vast gaping abyss without any kind of support. With much trepidation, Indy swallows hard and draws a deep breath. Undaunted, he wills himself to take the Leap forthwith. He is astonished to see a pathway appear below his feet. Indy casts a handful of sand onto the remainder of the path and confidently strides over it to the other side.

Now, perhaps more than ever before, we all face our own Leaps of Faith. But know that you are supported by the Living Light of God's love. Humanity is being re-programmed individually and collectively. We are to receive two additional chromosomes. Our human consciousness is being expanded and quickened to prepare us for the Great Spiritual Event to come.

Realize that the human reason constantly questions everything. The intellect wants to be certain, thus its facility in making sure that the stance we take in keeping with our belief. But to get closer to God, one must serve Him. Even the idea of service creates a conflict when we approach it using only the intellect. We ask how, when or where to express love for God and His creations. Rather, we must act on our intuitions, the inner promptings we feel, before the ego begins to question.

You may be told again and again that you are a child of God, a light bearer, a space being of the Ashtar Command, or a teacher of the mysteries responsible for teaching the "Word" of God. Put aside your questions and enter the light of courage and confidence. Realize that the spiritual and the physical are one. You and God are inseparable.

Be a light for your sisters and brothers. Speak the Truth as you know it from your heart. Many people hesitate to serve, waiting for God to personally give the Command of Action. But that day will never come. For truly, we gain confidence in ourselves by taking the smaller Leaps of Faith so that we can then take the larger ones.

I recall the way I learned to swim in my childhood. Our family spent our summers at the New Jersey shore, so I was given swimming lessons early on. The summer I was six years old I bravely ventured out into the tidal estuary because I wanted to get to the raft while the tide was out. At dead low tide I could walk all the way out to the raft with the water level varying between my thighs and my chest. I bravely walked through "the Drop", a slight deepening of the water halfway to the raft.

For hours I practiced jumping off the raft and stroking back to it, knowing I could touch bottom if necessary. The afternoon flew by as my fear vanished. I had forgotten that the tide would be coming in and the area around "the Drop" would be over my head. I found myself alone on the raft at high tide. All my friends had gone. In the distance I could hear my mother calling me home for dinner.

I felt very afraid to leave the raft. I looked at "the Drop" and imagined it to be a bottomless pit filled with all kinds of monsters. My heart raced and pounded in my chest. Then a gentle voice inside me said, "Go." All of my six years' old logic told me that I had no alternative but to take the "dive of Faith". I swam with all my might until I had crossed the monstrous "Drop" and felt the sand of the shore beneath me. In that moment I knew I could swim.

Our souls continuously push us forward in order to make us grow beyond the comfort zone of the human. The soul says: "Go out on the limb. Take the Leap of Faith." Then you can stand on the other side and proclaim, "I know that I know!"

"Look for the hero inside yourself.
Look for the good and loving heart
within you and everyone else.
Just as every seed holds the power
of creation within it
So do *you* and every other creature
in this world."

Ferngully (the movie)

An Open Letter from Jesus the Christ

Dear Beloved Brothers and Sisters,

Here it is October 20th, 1999, and we are on the precipice of a new millennium and a new era. But, as I reflect upon the approaching millennium and the one coming to a close, I feel it is important to address mankind via my emissary and dear brother in the light, John. I must say he was a bit reluctant to write this since his book, *Come the New Jerusalem,* was finished and ready for print. But I know this book will reach the hearts and souls of a great number of you. So be open and take what I am saying with an open mind and heart.

Sadly, where we stand at this point in man's history and the evolution of man as a collective whole has been slow and tedious. Yes, there is progress in individuals and groups, but overall the attitude of mankind is not much different than it was 2,000 years ago. The same forces that opposed me and the Almighty God exist today.

The Pharisees and Sadducees of old have been replaced by new faces, but their theme is the same. Man is sorely lacking in the fundamentals of spirituality needed to create the atmosphere which can facilitate their collective awakening. In this way they may embrace the universal principles of love, peace, and universal brotherhood and sisterhood.

Man has been seduced by the dogma of the many religions and held under the thumb of leaders acting as men of God but who are really men of political and material persuasion. They use my name in vain and have led many souls astray. They have been led away from their birthright to be eternally free in God. I urge you to be very discerning in matters of faith since there are so few true teachers out there. Always look within and learn to listen to your "still" voice which is your guide and your master teacher. Some of you have progressed nicely under the current spiritual dictatorship because you are pure in heart. God is omnipresent, omnipotent, and omniscient and therefore can help anyone anywhere. But for the average soul, the path has led them nowhere. And I feel for each and everyone of you and urge you to be independent and free and question where your pathway has led you. This is why I am writing this to all of you. To stand firmly in the knowledge that I, Jesus the Christ, am alive in all people, places, and things, regardless of the rhetoric that would tell you differently. I urge you to embrace all people as your extended spiritual family and not allow your religion to act as a wedge between you and your fellow human beings. Trust the Living Christ within you and then you will find me (Jesus) and all of the secrets you have longed to know.

Stay clear of being too dependent on psychics, channelling, and other things that border on the occult. There are people who are responsible mediums whose intention is pure and will not request that you come repeatedly for readings. Learn, dear ones, to trust yourself and the Great Spirit of Life which exists in everyone but which is mostly ignored.

I want to speak of the Ascended Host. Some of you are aware of these souls, but a great portion of the populace is sadly unaware of my brothers and sisters who attained their ascendancy. They assist my work as World Teacher and come from all traditions and pathways to help our Sovereign Father in his will to implement greater and greater programs of Light and Spiritual Evolution. The Christ is a universal energy and principle which is the foundation of all life. It doesn't belong to one tradition or religion but exists for everyone to participate in.

Do not reject other pathways that may or may not acknowledge me as the "Savior" or "Messiah." If other great teachers of the Ascended Host are leading people to the Light and the Christ within, that knowingness is one with me whether they make that statement or not. Do not judge, criticize, or condemn your fellows because your divine duty is to walk your pathway to the best of your ability. You are not to rebuke others because theirs is different from yours. Remember, *Love* and *Respect* are always the way, and it is the attitude of Love which will allow me to make my re-entry into matter along with the Ascended Host whose number is 144,000 strong!

Realize that my true teachings are only partially touched upon within your Bible so that you must go beyond your Book to find the truth of your being or spirit. God cannot be comprehended by the mind and the intellect alone. It is the purified heart that makes you like a little child once again, that enables you to unite with God. Do not doubt or rebuke God's messenger, John, for he, I, and all who love God are working together for the same thing: Peace, Joy, Freedom, and Abundance of every form for all of God's children. Amen.

Yours Truly in Love and Freedom for all.
Jesus the Christ.

Part V

Superconscious Mind

Humility, Not Self-Aggrandizement

IN THIS TIME OF PREPARATION for the Golden Age, many have jumped on the bandwagon of the "New Age Movement", promoting various consciousness-raising aids: crystals, homeopathics, radionics, astrological charts, healings, channelings, past-life regressions, retreats. These means of treatment, therapy and self-discovery are fine, but the leaders of these movements must realize true healing comes not from them, but from the I AM Presence. Jesus said. "Of myself, I AM nothing—it is all the will of the Father." As leaders and teachers, it is our duty to continually step aside, giving all credit to the Master within. We must put ourselves second and God first!

Great leaders realize they must first and foremost be the greatest disciples. We are forever disciples of the Most High Living God; we are *His* children, not the other way around. After all, who created whom? The path to higher consciousness is straight, narrow and as fine as a razor's edge. The ego wants us to use the power of God for our own ends—it especially tempts those in a leadership role. Great is the leader who can follow while leading, listen while guiding and always be open to suggestions, reveling in endless spiritual growth and ultimately adhering only to the voice of God within.

But how do we learn such humility? First we must obey, then we can command. But what, or whom, do we obey? On one hand, we each have a lower self rooted in ego, encompassing the body and its senses, characterized by hatred, pain, fear, separation and unrest. On the other hand, the God-Self, forever rooted in spirit, dwells in the heart center or "soul" and is characterized by love, compassion, courage, unity and peace.

By obeying and nurturing the God-Self, we can achieve true humility. False humility, put on to exemplify phony spiritual evolution, may convince some people but not our Creator. He knows our every thought and feeling, down to the subtlest nuance within our hearts. When we are ready to give all of ourselves to God, humility is a natural state and an essential part of our liberation. Only in humility does the eye remain single to God's glory.

Spiritual mastery requires discipline, practice, commitment and time, but if we work diligently and consistently our attainment will draw ever closer. It is far more valuable to be recognized by God than try to convince mankind of our worth. Attitudes change like the wind; what stability can we find in winning anyone over? Jesus said, "Seek ye first the kingdom of heaven," for that kingdom—and only that kingdom—can give us lasting satisfaction.

Self-Forgetfulness

THE ESSENCE OF SPIRITUALITY lies in self-forgetfulness. Little by little as we begin to remember, we forget about our limited selves. We begin to awaken the dreamer and touch the place of knowing that resonates deep inside our heart of hearts. That place inside each of us is filled with peace, balance, wisdom and boundless love.

Realize that there is no safe place on the physical plane save that of which I speak.

To lighten your load internally you can practice the beautiful exercise that follows. Visualize a flame or a fire in front of you. Place your earthly desires and attachments into that purifying fire.

A truly valiant spirit awaits the practitioner of self-forgetfulness. In this age of accelerated change there is a grand opportunity for those who are open to the process of evolution. Much of one's karma that has accumulated over many lifetimes may be consumed during this time of the quickening. The question is how to put aside earthly fears and doubts as we make decisions about where to live and how to store certain necessities for the coming times. The answer is *in giving*. As you give of yourself and see that each of us is a reflection of the other, you will help the whole grow in consciousness during this time of challenge.

All of your limitations lie in the pool of your lower self. All of your freedom lies in your spiritual self. Security will not be found in an outer safety net but in your inner connectedness with God. You make the choice!

The more you give of yourself, the more you will eat the fruit of the Divine. Giving is the bridge to self-forgetfulness. Give with love and joy so that you can release the hold which the small self has kept on you for countless rounds of birth, death and rebirth.

Jesus and the Ascended Host labor day and night to find people who will take on the Great Work. Invite your invisible brothers and sisters to commune with you and guide you. They may not violate your God-given free will. You must call on them yourself. As you make that call they will instruct you as to how you can serve God in humankind.

The more you open yourself to Truth and Love, the more you will be comfortable with the process. Remember always to invoke the mantra: "Kodoish, Kodoish, Kodoish Adonai 'Tsebayoth!" if you are invited to travel with one of the Host. This mantra will distinguish those of the true light from those masquerading as such.

You must not be naive about what is around us. You must remain alert. But learn to be calmly aware, rather than wary or guarded. Each and every one of you is protected. Remember: *the light of God never fails*. Trust in that support and play your part without hesitation.

Erase Egotism—Give All Credit to the Father

"OF MYSELF I CAN DO NOTHING; it is all the will of the Father." How many of us live by these words of Jesus? It is easy to get caught up in life's struggles and forget who is running the show.

Remember, God is the director. Everything belongs to Him—everything is His creation . Many of us are caught in our own illusory webs. We can be so full of our egos we have no room for God.

Little do we know that by ignoring God, we are turning our backs on the most important relationship of all—the one between us and our Creator. God has given us free will, the freedom to acknowledge Him or not. All of us need to ask how we have used the free will we've been given. Have we drawn closer to the Magic Presence each day, giving praise and adoration to God? Or have we created a world of selfishness and deceit, turning from life to embrace death? We must all choose, for we cannot have it both ways.

Just as children don't want to give up their toys, the childish ego within each of us doesn't want to let go of the pretense of ownership. The truth is we own nothing; all belongs to God—we are merely the caretakers of what we think of as ours. Search your heart of hearts and allow the light of your soul to penetrate this selfishness. Only when we let go of our attachment to God's gifts can we truly enjoy them. The more tightly we cling to false ownership, the more painful it becomes; materialism can own *us* if we let it.

All we can be sure of is the breath we are taking at this moment, nothing else. Let us offer that breath to the Father-Mother God. When we focus in this way, knowing our very lives are on loan, we can clearly see our spiritual path. Talk to God, sing His praises, seek to please Him. He waits for us to love Him unconditionally, not just when it's convenient and we remember to.

We can create a world of light here on earth if we acknowledge God in all His ways and are truly thankful for all He has given. If each of us would say: "Thy Will, not mine, be done," we could begin to align our hearts and minds as brothers and sisters of the Light.

Eradicate Fear and Doubt Through Transmutation

OFTEN WE FEAR what we do not understand. God, mysterious and unknown to us in any conventional sense, is usually looked upon with great trepidation. How do we remove the part of ourselves that clings to the known world and open ourselves to Him?

First, we must accept our fears and not run from them. By facing our fears, we begin to realize they are simply ideas triggered by our beliefs, superstitions and experiences. As we find the courage to walk through each manifestation of fear—indecision, lack of confidence and the rest—we begin to conquer them one by one.

It is said we can be our own best friends or our own worst enemies. How do we become our own best friends, our own teachers? We must learn to love every part of ourselves exactly as we are. By ignoring, enabling, or criticizing our weaknesses, we only reinforce them. If we can love them, we allow our spiritual light to be directed onto these areas of "dis-ease" within. This principle is known as the *law of transmutation*—using love to lighten the dark recesses of the unconscious and subconscious minds secretly ruling us. We rarely see the present moment *as it is*; we perceive it through our experiences, both positive and negative. As we slowly transmute these experiences, we begin to open to our superconscious or Christed Selves.

Life is completely different when viewed from the perspective of our God-selves. It is filled with joy, beauty, expansion, discovery and peace. It matters not that the pairs of opposites—good and evil, love and hate, ease and disease—still swirl around us. By balancing our reactions to life's ups and downs, we can be free of them.

We must begin to heal ourselves as we are! Let us befriend our fears, doubts, insecurities and anxieties, and accept them as loving parents except the foibles of their children. These hang-ups are *our* children—we have created them by identifying with our vulnerable egos rather than our perfect spirits. If we align ourselves with spirit, we will watch these undisciplined children become mature adults.

Life becomes unmanageable and full of conflict while we continue to dislike even a small part of ourselves. *If we love all of ourselves as we are, we will become masters of ourselves.* No guru, prophet or messiah can do it for us—they can only teach us by example. As great souls slay their personal dragons by loving them, we must allow the love of our Divine Selves to do the same, filling us and releasing our limitless potentials.

Before we go to sleep, we should list either silently or aloud the least-liked aspects of ourselves while expressing love for each of them. To fully energize our statements, we must breathe deeply. The breath then enters the dark chambers of our altered egos, our Anti-Christs. As our love energies react with the divine energies around us, we gain the momentum needed to begin healing the wounded parts of ourselves. We can then sleep deeply, filled with peace rather than emotional unrest.

We must begin to make this exercise part of our nightly routines, even if at times we might not feel up to it. If we persist, all our unconscious and subconscious blocks will eventually dissolve through the Law of Transmutation. We can each say, "*I (AM) love all parts of myself, and by loving them, I allow them to be healed and transmuted by the power of love.*" If we don't get immediate results, we must patiently continue to apply this law and ignore the doubting voices of our altered egos. The Law of Transmutation is the safest, surest and most effective way to empty ourselves so we may be filled with the Holy Spirit and attain salvation.

Meditation—Godly Food

MEDITATION, an extension of or close cousin to prayer, is our spiritual food. Many Western religions discourage this practice, associating it with Eastern methods such as yoga; but it is through meditation that we nurture the God-Self, allowing it to emerge by stilling the lower mind. In a sense, we are constantly meditating whether we are aware of it or not, for our God-Presence is silently guiding us if we choose to listen to it. However, it helps if we can create a quiet environment where we can more easily contact this part of us.

First, put on any relaxing music (many Classical and New Age selections are appropriate); soothing music will help you cross over from the empirical, concrete side of the brain to the more intuitive and creative side. Sit comfortably or lie down, but keep your spine straight; a straight spine allows spiritual currents to move freely. Next, completely focus on your breath, developing a rhythmic pattern; allow the breath to carry you deeper and deeper within yourself. As you begin to feel settled, visualize your passing thoughts as if they were clouds in the sky; just observe them without stopping or suppressing them. Find your inner center of peace and become rooted there, Let this sense of peace and love take you beyond any sense of limitation—this is the space of God within you.

If we listen closely to the still, small voice of the Father, He'll let us know how long we should meditate. As individuals, what may be too long for one may not be near enough time for another. It's important to keep making contact with this inner place; once we establish a relationship with our Higher Power, we'll always have somewhere to turn. God is our best friend, our beloved, our all-in-all. We must be tenacious in maintaining contact with Him, however, for the world holds many distractions that can mask our true heritage as His sons and daughters.

We must be aware of the possibility of drawing in negativity—not only while meditating, but at all times. We are in the Omega; the powerful transitions of the earth plane draw ever nearer. Now more than ever, darkness is fighting to keep its stranglehold over us. We must be careful, keeping in mind that God's voice is firm, supportive, compassionate and *always, always* loving.

Our ability to ward off negativity is greatly diminished if there is "dis-ease" in our systems; we are not able to function as our Creator intended. Meditation not only stills the mind, calms the emotions and slows the heart rate, but also helps heal the holes and cracks within our auras (the subtle energy fields surrounding our bodies), preventing negativity from entering.

Meditation is one of the greatest tools we have in our pursuit of God-realization. Used in conjunction with prayer, fasting and contemplation, it opens the windows to our souls, aligning our entire beings and allowing us to contact the peace within us all.

Meditation is something that you must be patient with. It is easy to understand the notion "be still and know that you are Gods and Goddesses." However, it is quite another matter to experience this within oneself. And it is the experience that is the greatest teacher of all. Fasting, practicing silence, reading of the scriptures, and the giving of oneself in selfless service help create the foundation or space within that allows God to be experienced directly within oneself. It is all a process or journey, to be experienced and not just intellectualized. So in whatever way you are seeking transcendence, remember the middle path will bring you success. Make your practice fun and allow it to be filled with joy. I always enjoyed my spiritual practice and quest and so I stuck with it. And as I began to experience the divine in "me" I was very glad I had approached it in this manner. Be steady and steadfast and at the same time enjoy your adventure. There are so many beautiful things to experience through your spirit that the time spent will not be in vain.

Now most of my time is spent in spontaneous and open-eyed meditation on different divine realities. The colors and sounds are so beautiful that there are no words to describe them in human terms. The unstruck sound, the Aum, the Great I-Am resonates in and around and through me ceaselessly depending on the time of day and my activity level. So keep on keeping on with your practice and don't get discouraged. The source (God) doesn't look to stay hidden from us but rather is us as we are this very moment. In stillness it becomes amplified and so is more easily discernible. One must transform the denser aspects of the personality into the finer elements of the soul. Once you accomplish this you begin to set the soul free. And once you know your freedom, you then can fully enjoy this journey we call Life.

Silence

BE STILL AND KNOW that you and God are one. Let silence draw you deep into the temple of your spirit. Enter the profound silence of that holy place and behold the true source of inner peace—your own divine Self.

For God's bond with you is unbreakable. Real love, God's love, is with you always, no matter what your circumstances. In God's presence there is only joy, light, peace and abundance. So anchor yourself deeply in spirit now.

Return to your silence when you are tempted to argue or engage in a debate. Silence will help you remain aware of the ego's tendency toward unnecessary speech. It will keep you closer to the real you, the spirit of God within yourself. It will also raise the consciousness of others you encounter.

The need for making stillness a greater part of one's daily life is truly important at this time.

In the early years of my spiritual discipline I set aside one day of the week for fasting and another for silence. At first it seemed more like a game than a discipline. When I needed to speak I simply wrote the message on a notepad.

In those days, I drove a school bus for junior and senior high school children. When I practiced silence I placed a sign near the steering wheel to instruct the children about my intentions. It was interesting to observe the day's activities from the perspective of a silent witness. Things went smoothly until one student took exception with my practice.

All of a sudden the child made a slighting comment and grabbed the back of my hair, forcibly pulling my head backward. I was provoked. My mood swiftly changed from serenity to annoyance and I broke my silence.

At first the students looked at me in surprise, but then we all shared a big laugh over the whole incident. Their play certainly succeeded in getting my attention. As I practiced silence more, I began to learn how to discriminate between the real world and the unreal world.

Silence let me be more in contact with the real me, the spirit of God within myself, and less caught in the foolish illusions of the ego. Silence brings you back to your original state in God; the free, unconditioned state you knew as a little child.

Witness a baby as it enters the world of human speech and learning. The baby sees the world through pure Spirit. The child remains in his purest state for the first year of his life knowing the world with innocent eyes and ears, with no terms for his direct experience. Gradually the child learns speech and begins to name his experiences. The more he develops speech, the more his awareness of spirit contracts. Thus, little by little we lose contact with pure divine consciousness.

Speech acts like a limiting mantra within our bodies. Its vibration resonates in a way that affects our perception of the world around us. Unconscious speech patterns keep us bound in a sense of separation from others.

I'm not suggesting that you should teach your child only the inner reality. Rather, I would encourage you to help him create a balance between the world of being close to God and the world of human concepts. Keep the spirit of your child awake. Share the secrets you are learning through your practice of silence so that you and your family can be more fully conscious of God's presence and love.

Practice this essential discipline with great love. Let life beckon you to learn by unlearning. Your senses will be keener. Your mind will be sharper. Your heart will be more open.

When you practice silence for a long time; when your energy is concentrated and whole; you can see into life. You can see more than may be seen by the naked eye. Go into nature and hear the sweet sounds, smell the delicate aromas and see the vibrant auras of plants and trees.

Let silence draw you into constant communion with the divine. Be still and hear the gentle voice of your soul. Know the free and joyful One who is forever calling in the altar of your heart.

Intuition

So often we have "gut feelings" about people, places and events past, present and future. First impressions and deep feelings come from an inner voice—the intuition. Because of its subtlety, intuition is often overlooked and easily misunderstood. If acknowledged it all, it is usually underused and underrated. Once we being to follow it, however, we find intuition is a God-given ability that helps attune us to our deeper impulses.

Essentially we have two inner voices. One is the loud, limiting voice of the altered ego. It judges, fears and creates anxiety. It is pompous, arrogant, willful and can only love its own miscreation. Worst of all, this voice masks our Divine Selves, stealing our peace, happiness and potential for higher experience in the process. Unfortunately, this voice is master of most of us.

In order to free ourselves from this voice, it must be silenced. First, simply witness it—hear it for what it is. This is very tricky, since our loud ego-driven voices seem so much a part of us and are so often heard by us that we don't consider them harmful. We may each be thinking, "This is what I'm used to. What's all the fuss about?" Someday we will have an answer for our choices; thus, we must continually work to break free of the traps that our altered egos set for us.

Thankfully, each of us also has an intuition, a still, small voice that is part of the Divine Mind. It is our lifeline to God, and His way of making sure His children stay on the path leading back to Him. Our intuitions speak for the parts of us that are loving, forgiving, selfless, caring and content in and of themselves. This voice, the Master Presence in us all, will always love us as we are and guide us throughout our lives.

God has given the gift of Himself to us; He has given us His essence in a form unique to each of us. We are his sons and daughters, but so few of us have taken the time to live up to our birthright by developing confidence in the voice of God within. We *must* learn to trust the insights of our Higher Minds! The light of God never fails and *we are that light*. Our intuitions allow us to brightly shine God's light on all we do.

It would be interesting to keep an "Intuition Diary." In it, we would note each experience, the voice we listened to when we contemplated the experience and the result of the action taken. What happened when we followed our altered egos' advice? What about when we listed to our intuitions? Did we consistently follow one voice or the other?

The highest truth is to be true to God within us—when we stray from this, pain is the only result. Following our intuitions takes discipline at first, but gradually becomes easier and more natural. With quiet intensity and dedication to the Father, we can overcome any obstacle we have created.

Each of our lives has a divine blueprint showing our pathways home to God. To follow these paths, we must each surrender to the Divine Will that speaks through our intuitions. The more we resist our higher callings, the more difficult our lives become. We must let all illusion go and open our hears to the Father-Mother God within, following the searchlights of our souls as they illuminate our destinies.

Be As Gentle As a Dove and As Clever As a Serpent

As we walk in this world of ever changing circumstances and realities, it is important to remember: "Be gentle as a dove and as clever as a serpent." As we open our hearts to God and feel His Love dance through every cell within us, we must be mindful to discriminate between the real and the true- the light, and the unreal, the false- the dark. As you open your heart to love, you must not be so blinded by this love that you lose sight of the deceptions and masquerades of darkness.

Jesus said many false prophets shall arise to fool even the chosen ones. This is why you must use your power of discrimination and trust your gut feelings. All of us have that barometer of knowing within ourselves that helps us discern between the light and the dark. Here are seven characteristics of the Light:

1. The Power of the Light is always loving.
   In fact, it is the power of Love itself.

2. The Power of the Light is always humble.
   Yet through humility you will be shown your true power in God.

3. The Light is never controlling.
   It will never violate your free will, but will suggest the course of action to be taken.
   (The choice is yours.)

4. The Light is never boastful, jealous, envious, lustful, greedy or angry. It knows its source is God.

5. The Light will never manipulate your life in a way that causes you to go against your family or your friends or your associations in the world. For all are one and all is Love!

6. The Light will never demand large sums of money to teach you its ways. Rather, it will help you afford all the tools you need for your growth.

7. The Light will constantly uplift you and give you the strength, courage, love, wisdom and power to fulfill your mission in life. The Light will accelerate your energy, your love, your abundance, your wisdom and your power to go forward despite the human tendency to stop, consider and weigh all the possibilities. This is where Faith comes in. Faith is the bridge that connects the finite and the infinite, the known and the unknown, the visible and the invisible.

Remember these seven qualifications as you encounter "teachers" on the pathway homeward. Anyone who attempts to seduce, control or dominate you in any way that strips you of your God-given birthright is not of the Light.

As people grow in Spirit they may feel the doubts, the confusion and the fears of their human sheaths. In this stage of development one can be very vulnerable. Be careful not to be misled by any person who assumes the role of God. A teacher of the Light will help you get in touch with *your* dominion in and through God and will assist *your* Quickening.

Be very alert in this time of the Quickening and keep in mind these seven Golden Rules of True Spiritual Conduct. They will help you to be "as gentle as a dove and as clever as a serpent." To find your way back home you will need both of these qualities and more.

God bless you all! Amen.

Open Minds, Open Hearts

Opening people's minds to their God-Selves is one of the most important and difficult tasks ahead. Although most of us consider ourselves to be open-minded, we cling to aspects of negative conditioning as if our lives depended on them. Actually, our lives depend on the *release* of all concepts and ideas that block our love essences.

Watch young children. They'll get angry for a moment, but in the next moment, after forgiving and forgetting, they'll play harmoniously like nothing happened. What an example for adults! God wants our expression of love to be as free and unlimited as a child's. "Unless you be like a little child, you shall not enter the kingdom of heaven," Jesus said.

Brothers and Sisters of the Light, the truth is not found in our ego-filled minds but in the spirit-filled hearts *behind* our minds! We are united under God, even though the pull of the ego makes us feel isolated from one another. Our egos feed this sense of isolation by making us feel superior sometimes and inferior at others, but how can we be both? And how can my God-Self be superior or inferior to yours? Cast off the influence of the ego once and for all, for it masks who we really are—*one heart, one mind, one energy, God incarnate*.

As the ego loses its grip, the mind opens effortlessly. Love surges from the heart, intoxicating us with its power so that we can love our fellow man unconditionally, without judgement. But it takes time to break the ego's hold; thus, persistence and determination are important for spiritual seekers. If we set out wills toward enlightenment, the Divine Will guides us with ease. As we will, so will it be.

As we undergo our tests and trials, we must remember the example of Jesus. No matter what He endured, He never gave up. Don't think that because He knew Himself to be the Messiah, the Son of Man, that it made continuing on in the face of adversity any easier. Jesus conquered the pull of the flesh because He wanted liberation more than anything else. If we cultivate the same yearning in our open minds and hearts, nothing can stop us, for *the Light of God never fails*.

The Group Mind Dynamic

W<small>E ARE ALL ONE MIND</small>—God mind—but our misperceptions keep us from this knowledge. Because we forget that we are all one mind, we create not only our personal problems but problems for the world as well. How do we overcome these delusions and live by our true natures?

As we still the lower mind, we open ourselves to the Divine Mind. Heaven and hell, birth and death and all pairs of opposites are experienced by the lower mind. If we could only gain control of it, we would discover who we really are—pure spirit, forever free, connected to the Father-Mother God in the fullness of our beings.

Positive affirmations are a dynamic way to raise the vibration of the lower self. As we continually affirm the I AM, the Higher Self, we allow God to break the web of illusion that is the lower mind. Use these affirmations, saying them aloud:

1) I am God, God am I.
2) I am the perfect manifestation of my world at this very moment.
3) I am the perfection of God in action.

As these words are spoken and their meanings contemplated, we begin to understand our true nature. We must never feel we are not worthy of this realization—it is our birthright as children of God. We cannot buy into the negative suggestions of our minds and of the world around us. Instead, we should seek unlimited love and prosperity. It takes time to break the chains of negative thought, so we must continue to affirm our spiritual essence until our lower selves no longer bind us.

As more of us begin to live by the Group God-Mind ideal, we will release what our spirits have longed to express. If we could get beyond the constraints of our lower minds, we would naturally love and care for each other. We would realize we *are* each other. In God we are one, in spirit we are one, in truth we are one. Through the Group God-Mind we can directly experience this oneness. An Eastern scripture states, "He who thinks he knows, knows not, and he who thinks he knows not, knows." Our lower minds think separation is truth, that there is no Group God-Mind—but our spirits know better. Each of us must break these chains of darkness and ignorance, allowing the inner light of God to shine through.

God speaks to us through our still, small voices. If our hearts and minds are receptive, we will hear the Father's advice and direction on a day-to-day basis. If we faithfully follow God's word, this world will evolve beyond anything our lower minds could imagine. *Faith does move mountains!*

We are one group mind in God; as we acknowledge this oneness, we see we are not meant to live in pain and sorrow, but in joy and happiness. Let us walk through the fires of life with our heads held high, our resolves firm and our hearts filled with love, until the day all of our dreams are realized.

Give Up Being Right and Be at Peace

Each of us has a shallow surface mind generated by our egos. The surface mind is opinionated, judgmental, critical and, above all, loves to be right! For example, in spiritual matters, we each tend to see our own path as the right one, the only one to save mankind. Spirituality is a very personal subject, and we must each have a chance to learn of it and experience it for ourselves in the privacy of our own hearts.

Peace is our natural state. If we would devote as much time to cultivating peace as we do to debating and arguing about whose truth is truer, the world would surely be a different place. Most of us are seeking peace and don't even know it; in financial security, in the emotional contentment of relationships and in the satisfaction that comes from the ownership of material things. Some of us try to numb ourselves into a peaceful state with drugs or alcohol. None of these substitutes, however, can replace the inner peace that we have lost somewhere along the way.

The only true and lasting peace, in this world or any other, is found in our souls. Beneath the noise of the surface mind there is a hidden treasure that shows us our true selves. We are not sense-slaves that exist simply to desire and gratify those desires—we are vast creatures of light, limitless in our expressions of life and truth. To learn our true natures, we must ignore the judgment of our egos. Peace is the gateway to heaven, the foundation of all spiritual attainment. To achieve it, we must train ourselves to break the holds our surface minds have on us.

One way to begin retraining the surface mind is by observing all we think, do or say in a detached manner. We have two distinct natures: the ego or surface mind lives and reacts, while the spirit or God-Mind silently witnesses the play of the ego while remaining unattached to it. Our perfect, loving spirits, unmoved by life's up and downs, wait to be acknowledged as our true gateways to freedom. Jesus said, "Seek ye first the kingdom of heaven." Heaven exists on earth in a peaceful heart—a caring, courageous heart unafraid to make a mistake or to say the wrong thing. We are each beings of human imperfection and spiritual perfection; nothing need be added to us, but our humanness must gradually set aside and allow our spirituality to express itself. Deep down, we all want to love, to be loved and to feel "peace that passeth all understanding."

Another way to overcome the lower mind is to replace negative thought with positive God-thought. We must train the mind to think correctly; it will resist at first, but will follow the lead of God within. Remember, spirit has created mind, not vice versa. By opening to God, the surface mind begins to lose its hold over us.

There is no true and lasting happiness in the world; everything fades away like a passing image across the grand screen of life. We pay too much attention to these projected images and not enough to the projector—God. We should take a step back, for we are usually too close to the action to see what's *really* happening in our lives. Let's be still, have fun and watch our lives unfold before us.

As we give up the ego's need to be right, we can begin to learn the lessons of spirit; our lower minds step aside and let the perfection and peace of our Higher Selves shine through. Recognizing spirit as our essence, we can work each day toward taking our place in God's eternal family of man.

Illusion Creates Confusion

WE CREATE THE REALITY OF OUR LIVES by our reactions to each day's events. When we are happy with the day, we feel contented; when the day is frustrating and unsatisfying, we tend to become unfocused, detaching from our negative experiences. This is unfortunate, for we must be in touch with our Higher Selves in order to understand that the sense-world, the world of circumstance we create and consider real, is an illusion. Many of us are so ensnared by this illusion there is no room for anything else, including God, in our minds and hearts.

The earth is the plane of the senses and we must exist upon it; but to truly live on all levels, we should focus on the animating spirit of life rather than simply on sense perception. When freed from the boundaries of the senses, we see that we can achieve many levels of expression. We begin to live for God instead of letting our souls lie dormant, helpless in the face of the lower self's physical dependency.

The play of the senses consists of ups and downs—profit and loss, praise and blame, all pairs of opposites. Since we can't really control these cycles, confusion abounds on this planet. Those that are cut off from their Higher Selves inflict pain on themselves and others; there is no peace in their hearts. As Phil Collins of Genesis sings, surely "this is a *Land of Confusion*".

Fortunately, there is a way out. We need only draw ourselves into the silence of our beings four or five times a day, for five minutes each time, to gain repose. Thus we can rest in the Holy Spirit, the great comforter, the only lasting peace on the earth plane. In stillness, we quiet our minds and focus at the point between the eyebrows. The images seen through this, the "third eye", show us *true* reality; once we widen our sight in this way, our sense of physical vision will never be the same. This is why holy men and women have always been called "seers"; they can discern the truth in anything, seeing it for what it is.

    We will never find deep and lasting peace in this world. People, places and things come and go; everything is constantly in flux. We must look away from the world and its illusions, seeking instead the kingdom of heaven within. Then we will remember the difference between the outer physical world of illusion and the inner spiritual world, never again being confused as to where reality lies. By finding heaven, the sleeping dreamer in each of us will surely awaken!

We Are Creating the Apocalypse

WE ARE CREATING THE APOCALYPSE that is upon us! Many of us have read, heard and spoken so much about the traumatic events to come; we don't realize that all this attention is actually bringing the painful changes we fear into being!

Remember, nothing is etched in stone. If we see the world as perfect in our mind's eye, picturing it as whole and free of discord, the resulting positive God-energy can actually be a transmuting force helping us avert destruction. This force must be spread and shared; love and positivity must be networked on a large scale. We can't sit back and feel content in the serenity of our homes. Instead, we must open our doors wide, for only together do we have a chance to lessen the impact of the cataclysms ready to sweep the earth.

None of us, not even scholars of the Bible, Edgar Cayce or Nostradamus, has an inkling of God's Will, so we shouldn't be either fatalistic or blase about what is to come. Though we realize there is no death for the soul, each of us will be physically parted from loved ones somewhere along the line; therefore, we shouldn't wait until the last moment to join our minds and hearts as one energy. On the other hand, sometimes people speak so indifferently of earth changes, it seems they're going to watch the movies "Earthquake" and the "Poseidon Adventure" while the *real* script unfolds. This is *serious business*. If we don't make drastic changes it won't be a picnic here on earth!

While the earth is the focus of the positive energy of the entire universe, only our collective consciousness at the moment of planetary change will determine the intensity of the change we endure. We must wake up *now*, not because of fear but because of the desire to fulfill our great potential for love and fellowship. If we stand firm and true in spirit, we can band together and insure our survival through the Apocalypse and beyond.

It is important to understand the nature of prophecy to realize the part that it plays in predicting the future. A prophecy is a possibility or even a probability but not a certainty. What actually happens depends upon us. We know the world must change in order for many of the ancient prophecies to be averted. We have a choice in all of this! However, if we continue down the selfsame path of separation, egotism, and selfishness, one by one the prophecies of old will come to pass. The message is quite simple: we must change from a materially centered people to a spiritually centered one.

The Hopi prophecy rock shows man clearly having two distinct destinies. One, that of ego and otherness, will create a future of destruction and cataclysm. The other one of Love, Brotherhood, and Sisterhood will create an entirely new world and destiny for all mankind. I hope with all of my heart that we choose the latter and not the former. Realize that each and everyone is capable of so much good by the very power and content of your thought. Affirm the power of God within you and see it in everyone and everything for that is the truth of all existence. We have the power to direct the course of Earth history by our Love. Don't give in to prophecy, thinking that this is the way it is and it cannot be changed. We hold the world in our hands and the keys to its collective destiny will be determined by our collective Love or negatively by our collective apathy, fear, and separation. Let us break down the walls that have long held us back from our true identities and by so doing create the *New Jerusalem* through the high road of peace, Love, and harmony. Amen.

Channeling:
Its Use and Misuse

CHANNELING HAS BECOME very popular in this, the age of the Holy Spirit. We want to know about ourselves; our purposes, our relationships, any aspects of ourselves we want to more fully understand. As we grow spiritually, it can be very helpful to work with a person who interprets messages and receives information from a member of the angelic kingdom, a spirit guide or one of the Ascended Host.

The Brotherhood of Light is always looking for *proper* channels to help better prepare us and enlighten us as to our purposes and potentialities in God. Mother Earth is making her transition; since there is much confusion and little time to prepare for the trials that lie ahead, it is no surprise that many seek to be spiritually quickened by information obtained through channelers. Being wary of the faddish nature of this practice, we should first carefully examine the credibility of the channeler and the entity being channeled.

It takes twelve years to prepare a person to channel, according to the Brotherhood of Light. He or she must be mentally and emotionally clear, as well as spiritually mature, in order to allow full and unbiased transmission of an outside voice. In addition, an entity other than the particular one being channeled can influence a reading. Just as there is a Brotherhood of Light, there is also a brotherhood of darkness that can infiltrate the channeling, creating distortions and false predictions that could alter the life of the person heeding the tainted information.

We must be as vigilant regarding channeled information as we are with information from any other source, and use our God-given abilities to discern what is true and what is false. Some people automatically regard their entire reading as truth from God Almighty. No channeling, no matter how gifted the medium, can ever be one hundred percent correct! People change, energies change. Everything is in such constant flux that we must rely solely on ourselves for the truth. If we must know something, we should ask God for a sign and have patience—the answer will come in His time, not ours.

Often it is our anxieties, doubts and fears that cause us to pursue such information. Do we really need to know who we might have been in the time of Christ? Such knowledge can hurt rather than help; there is no more dangerous enemy than one's over-inflated spiritual ego. Why lose ourselves in the past? By the grace of the Father, we are gods and goddesses right now!

We give up the power of our birthright when we rely on another for that which is in us. If we are patient, still, and live in God, all things will come to us. Trust in God's love. Seek His truth sincerely and faithfully, not out of desperation. The kingdom of heaven lies within us and we must open the doorway to it. No one can do it for us, no matter how gifted he or she may be.

True channeling should only be done under controlled circumstances. Tuella, a gifted messenger of the Brotherhood of Light, was directed to specific sites at specific times to receive the information she dispensed through her books. There is much money to be made in channeling, of course, so there is no shortage of self-appointed spokespersons who command large fees for readings with the various entities they channel. For these careless spokespersons, the selection of site and time or their own readiness to receive messages are of little or no concern—their primary interest is money, not the quality or the clarity of the information received.

With love, I urge everyone to gain strength and courage from the voice of God within. There is no greater teacher for each of us than ourselves. We must trust ourselves above all and keep the pathway to God open waiting on His will. Jesus said, "*Knock and the door shall be opened; ask and it shall be given to you.*" Be patient—all things will be revealed in God's time.

The Role of the Guru

IN THIS AGE OF SPIRITUAL TRANSFORMATION, gurus (a Sanskrit word meaning "teachers") have emerged to help lead people safely across the ocean of worldliness. While many of us need this guidance, often a guru becomes *too* important. The role of any spiritual teacher is to assist a student in contacting his or her Higher Self. But worshiping a teacher as a divine being can be very dangerous to teacher and student alike.

Our Creator is the only one worthy of our highest devotion—no human guru, no matter how evolved the soul, deserves the same. Even Jesus, one of the greatest teachers of all, reminded His disciples, "Of myself I AM nothing; it is all the will of the Father." All true gurus shun the pedestal their followers would put them on, deflecting praise to the Most High Living God. Until they ascend as Jesus did, leaving their physical bodies behind, they exhibit the same human frailties and are subject to the same temptations as anyone else. We should love and respect these teachers who mirror our divinity, yet reserve total devotion for God the Father alone.

As lazy, hero-worshipping spiritual seekers, we have ruined many genuinely helpful paths ourselves. No one can do our work for us; great teachers assist us by doing nothing. Although it is true that the high vibration of a guru's soul can cause a disciple's spiritual experiences to be more powerful in the guru's presence, the energy comes from *God*, not the guru. Since a guru is but a channel for God's spiritual power and love, why not honor the source? By worshipping God directly, we will experience great ecstasy whether in the guru's presence or not.

When we do rely too heavily on gurus, we tend to adopt a holier attitude in their presence than the one we maintain in everyday life. True gurus show us who we really are *all* the time; we don't mysteriously change upon leaving them! With this understanding, we won't lose the blissful feeling found with our gurus.

Besides meaning teacher, guru also means "from darkness" (gu) "to light" (ru). Thus, the goal of our work with a spiritual teacher is to remove the darkness of the lower mind, allowing the light and clarity of the God-Mind to emerge. Why return lifetime after lifetime if we can do this work *right now*? A teacher can inspire, but we must perspire.

Gurus can provide much of the spiritual upliftment needed in this dawn of the Golden Age, but it is up to us to avoid the pitfalls that lead to the misuse of this great resource. A true teacher mirrors God's light; we must accept what is reflected back to us, making ourselves fertile earth so that seeds planted by God's messengers bear abundant fruit. With honor and respect for the teacher in each of us, let us devote our lives to the Ancient One who simply asks that we love Him as He loves us.

United We Stand, Divided We Fall

This is a call to the Children of the Light to band together and become one mind, one heart. This universal mind-heart is the spirit of God within us all. While each of us may have a different purpose or assignment, it is extremely important to recognize the overall plan and concentrate our energies in support of it. God merely asks us to love and respect each other as He loves and respects us. The petty ego battles between souls must cease; it is time for us to practice what we preach and live what we teach.

Our strength lies in unity; remember, a house divided cannot stand. We must try to let go of all that separates us from our brothers and sisters; this excess baggage is unnecessary. As soon as we remove these barriers and stop judging each other, we can begin to live and work together. Many of us want to be told about ourselves in channelings and other psychic readings, but we must try to draw our own spiritual conclusions. We are all God's children, so let's drop the spiritual and intellectual pride and the false faces that divide us. We are being tested, and we pass or fail by either holding onto or letting go of whatever stands in the way of love.

In the world of sports, great teams possess the qualities of self-sacrifice, unity and persistence; God's vast volunteer army must have the same. Many trials await us as God's soldiers, for we must help those not yet enlisted turn to the light rather than to darkness. It is more important than ever for each of us to overcome the fears and illusions generated by the lower self. We of the light can defeat this dark force by dedicating our lives to the Christ Consciousness. Whenever the lower mind seeks to control us, we should simply say, "*God I AM.*" Though this statement affirms that we are all gods and goddesses, it also points out that we are dependent on God the Father for life and salvation.

As Children of the Light, each of us must assume his or her spiritual responsibility; shirking this duty would only increase the burdens of those who are fulfilling their obligations. To begin the work we are meant to do, we must first overcome our fears. While conquering these anxieties might seem to be an overwhelming chore, all the help we need will come from God if we just ask. God is forever helping us if we allow ourselves to be helped; through Him we can become fearless, confident that nothing can infiltrate our armor of light and love unless we allow it.

The choice is ours—we can either obey the will of the Father and work together to create heaven on earth, or continue to live our isolated lives and watch the planet destroy itself. Let us think and feel as one, forever ready to uphold each other as we shine our light upon the darkness in this, the time of the Omega.

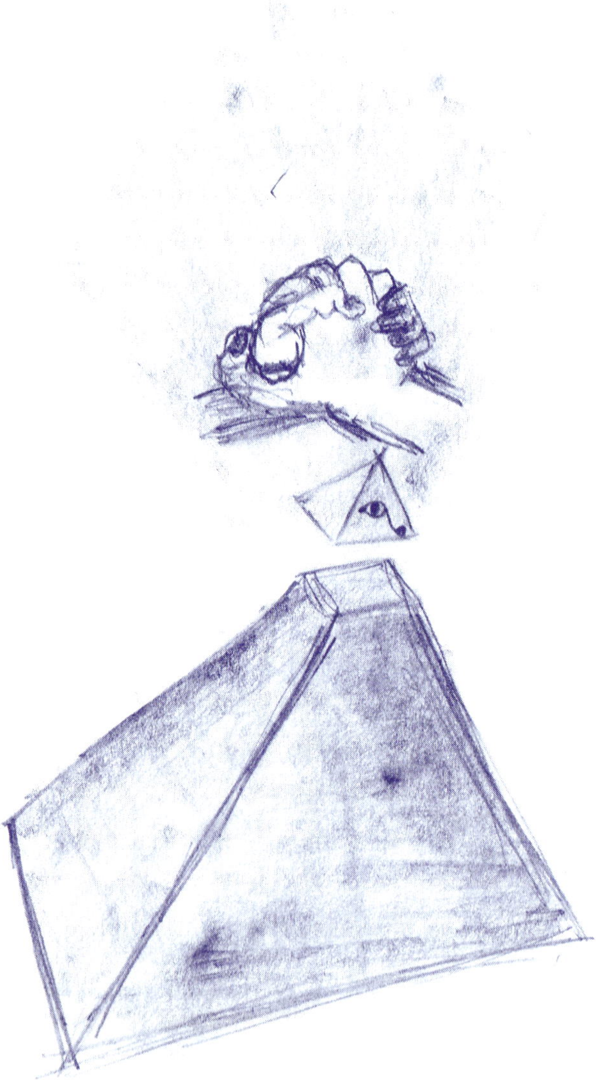

The Attention

*A*S A MAN THINKETH, *so will he be*. The attention is probably the least known yet the most important aspect of the make-up of our consciousness. Basically, the whole art of living spiritually consists in keeping one's attention on God. In the following pages you will find disciplines for living spiritually that will help you learn to control the internal dialogue; the conversation you have with yourself. Then you can expect to plunge deeper into the stillness in order to hear the still, small voice of your creator. After that, your concentration truly deepens with practice. You can begin to ignore the distracting voices of fear, doubt, envy, disappointment and so on.

Essentially, there are two strategies for managing negative emotions. One is to let the feeling pass through you without acting on it. The other is to replace the negative emotion with a positive one. Especially practice forgiveness.

As you learn to control the internal dialogue, your attention can stand guard over your thoughts. It will grow stronger and more firmly centered on God. Think of your awareness as a short-wave radio. The attention is the antenna or the mechanism by which you, as the operator, control the messages you want to receive or send. The greater your concentration, stillness and serenity, the deeper the level at which your attention makes contact with the Source. One never forgets the experience of touching and being touched by the Source.

On the bird of self-realization there are two wings: self-effort and grace. As you increase your effort in your daily life you will become more connected to God. After the attention has been entirely fixed at the center of your being, eventually there comes the realization of the word (see *The Power Of The Word*) and the realization of other manifestations of Light. Effort then gives way to Grace, a ceaseless flow of light, sound, and bliss.

> "This light is the Living Love which outshines all darkness, so that the darkness can never put out the *Word*, the light code in the midst of our "tree of life" as the Living Light. And as much as you have humbled yourselves before God, the blessings of His language of Living Light will shine into the heart of every soul you touch and heal with His Word, for the Lord is Adonai Shammah- the Lord is here in this hour in His Word which is implanted in you! Amen, Amen, and Amen."
>
> "Key of Enoch", by J. J. Hurtak pg. 466

Realize that we do nothing by ourselves. Really it is God, through the Word—the Living Light—who works through us. In truth, to be a disciple is to know and love discipline. Everyday now I hear the sweet sound of the Word. This is the awesome power that has enabled me to forge ahead through adversity and disappointment.

In summary, place your attention on the center of your being. Don't allow your mind to wander into negative thoughts and feelings, but direct it back to its Source. Discipline yourself. Concentrate on using your attention to get closer to God. Be a beacon of light and show your brothers and sisters the way by the example of your life.

"Live simply so others can simply live."

Part VI

Multi-Dimensional Spirit

Whispers from the Silence

ALL AROUND US IS LOVE. Pure, exquisite, ecstatic and soothing. As we sit quietly we can feel the closeness of our gentle brothers and sisters, the Ascended Host. They are all about us, serving as our link from the finite world of incarnation to the infinite world we will move into after we exit. Behind, beside and before us, these gentle beings are guiding, inspiring and protecting us in all that we do.

The Ascended Masters kindly help assist our individual and collective processes of evolvement. They are aware that it is difficult to be incarnated during this era. Our humanness wants to live in the known and familiar ways.

We hear about earth changes, shifting of the axis, space ships evacuating people from danger zones, and the quickening of spiritual consciousness—all culminating in a glorious Golden Age. But while we are glad in our spirits about the hope of a new tomorrow, even an age of true enlightenment, the human side still doubts, questions and wonders how our friends and families will fare through the coming times. We feel a bit fragmented in the process.

The Ascended Host is cognizant of our dilemmas. They know our strengths and weaknesses. In actuality, they know us better than we know ourselves. They also know the innermost longings of our heart of hearts. They ceaselessly help remind us of who we really are, what we agreed to do, and how to implement our missions.

Call to your gentle brothers and sisters, for they are with us always; always they are helping us get out of our own way.

As you truly love and trust God, you attract His Emissaries of Love and Light. With a humble heart bursting with love of life, love of truth and love for each other, ask these beloved whole light beings to walk with you. The legion of Ascended Masters wants to link closely with all of us. There is no separation between the physical and the spiritual, the real and the unreal, the substance and its shadow—all is one! It is this oneness or unity that we all seek to remember. It is the remembrance of a time when everything existed in the ambrosia of the one. A time of pure joy, pure love, wisdom, power and guilelessness.

Meditate and pray and remember. It is your birthright and your destiny. As each one sees the New Jerusalem in their mind's eye, it shall be done. For this is a truth that was conceived and fostered by God millions of years ago. Together, we are the collective mid-wives who will witness and assist its glorious birth.

Call to your gentle brothers and sisters. Always go into the silence. Forever listen to the whispers. Hear the still, small voice of God and His ascended children. Realize that many of you are ascended children who chose to be here to play your part. Stand up fearlessly. Hold the sword of Michael overhead and proclaim God's Kingdom on earth, the New Jerusalem.

Surrender to God's Will

IN THE *LORD'S PRAYER* Jesus proclaims, "Thy kingdom come, Thy will be done, on earth as it is in heaven." Though many of us have recited this prayer over and over, few have acknowledged the importance of Divine Will as a constant source of strength and guidance from God. We are more familiar with free will, a gift God has given each of us so we might come to Him of our own accord. The world is in its precarious state, however, as a result of our selfish misuse of free will and ignorance of Divine Will.

God wants to see His children live in peace regardless of racial, political or religious differences. Is unconditional acceptance of our fellow man too much to ask? Common sense tells us this is the only way to ensure our survival; continued disharmony will only hasten and intensify the coming earth changes.

We should each take an honest look at ourselves and begin to refine the doggedly ignorant parts of us. Our everyday conduct is very important. Each time we argue with an erratic driver on the road, scream at a slow person at the checkout counter or use an ethnic slur, we add to the ugliness and hatred that is ruining this beautiful world. *We* are responsible, by our hurtful attitudes toward one another, for the Armageddon we are about to face.

Beneath its skyscrapers and cement, the earth is a living, breathing entity; it can no longer tolerate the folly existing on its surface. While we continue on our destructive course, the rest of the universe waits for us to catch up to the examples set by other worlds. When Jesus said, "There are many mansions in my Father's house," He was referring to the multitude of worlds existing between earth and heaven—harmonious worlds without governments, religions or any other paranoid institution created by man's lower self. As mankind rises in consciousness, we will be self-governing, following only the will of our Creator. To achieve the fullness of our heavenly destiny on earth, there must be a deep spiritual revolution within the hearts and minds of each of us *right now*.

In my travels, I've observed that the majority of people seem to want sweeping spiritual change but are too afraid to express it; they are reluctant to give up their meager existences. As Jesus said, "He who holds onto his life shall lose it, and he who loses his life in My Name shall find it." The fear of death and the desire to cling to the body limit and eventually kill us. Flesh must perish, so why don't we live for our spirits and taste the immortality that is everyone's birthright?

We must *surrender* to the part of us that loves unconditionally ... that understands ... that has compassion, courage and strength ... that has the resolve to press on amidst adversity. We can choose to obey this part of us, the Christ Consciousness, or give in to the lower mind. Every decision is important, for each positive response helps raise the vibration of our world.

United as one Divine Mind, we can be a strong force effecting great change—if we all play our parts. We must carry the torch of truth and light to our brothers and sisters and help arouse that which is awakening in us. Let us recognize the divine spark in one another and live for the good of the whole.

Learning to Trust God

It often seems we walk down life's pathways alone. The perception is that we come alone and that we go alone, but in truth we are never alone. If we look behind the scenes, God is always with us, showering us with His love and grace. But how to we learn to contact God so we can trust His presence and know implicitly that we are in touch with Him?

We are the garden of the Holy Spirit. Like a garden, we must cultivate our hearts to receive the seeds of our Lord. We can do this by having an unbiased attitude, ready to receive the seeds of faith, hope and charity. We can then fertilize these attitudes with a sense of love and appreciation for all things, and they will grow. But can these attitudes also grow from adversity?

Adversity raises many questions. For instance, how do we deal with anger when it is being directed at us? Do we fight back or submit passively because we don't want to make waves? In a heated discussion, silence indicates complicity. How do we stand our ground without merely getting into a shouting match?

In order to hear God's voice in this kind of situation, we must stay calm; if we can maintain our equilibrium, insight will come. We will be able to take responsibility for our part of the argument and step back from the spillover of past frustrations and extenuating circumstances. We must trust our Higher Selves, which will lead us through turbulent moments by increasing our understanding and filling us with compassion. Fighting fire with fire just creates a larger, more dangerous fire; it's a no-win situation. "Yield and overcome", says Lao-Tsu in the Tao Te Ching. By overcoming the ego's desire to be right, we allow the wisdom and peace of the soul to come through. We surrender to God's will and *listen* to His voice.

Realize that God is love; He shows us gentleness, forgiveness, kindness, wisdom, strength and courage even in the face of our worst experiences. We must be open to His voice, for we cannot fully experience His love if we only do what we want—we must surrender to His direction. Giving everything to God requires self-control, but in the end it lifts us higher and higher.

Obeying God the Father is easy when we know in our hearts that He is working in our best spiritual interest. When we feel ourselves getting upset, we need only control our egos so that the God-Force can hold us in Its eternal embrace.

All Paths Lead to God

ALL PATHS LEAD TO GOD; their variety and number allow us each to express Divine Love in his or her own way. Some of us focus mostly on devotion to God; others of an intellectual bent pursue the pathway of knowledge; still others prefer to actively serve mankind. Those of us not predisposed to any of these expressions will utilize them all in combination. Still, most of us will be directed by a Divine Ray specifically associated with our strongest tendency.

Each of us is drawn to a religion or belief system in alignment with his or her particular ray or path. However, today's religions have strayed far from the truths on which they were founded and consist mostly of man-made ideas intended to illustrate one path's superiority over another. Since every path leads to the one light, one love, one energy we call God, there is really no difference among them; all are simply stepping stones to God-realization.

Many of us dogmatically cling to our beliefs, rejecting the idea that what works for us might not necessarily work for others. So we preach, thinking we have found the magic formula for spiritual and worldly success when we are just trying to reinforce our shaky belief systems. If we are secure in ourselves and our beliefs, we won't feel the need to give a "Sermon on the Mount" to everyone that comes our way. Remember, silence is golden, and the thing most given yet least wanted is advice!

We all must learn to lead by example. As we develop the ability to listen to our fellow travelers, we allow them to make their own choices. By unblocking ourselves, we invite God to move through us freely; *then* we can worry about unblocking others!

As we walk our allotted paths, we must ignore those who seek to convince us that their way is the only true salvation. Salvation will come to anyone—Christian, Jew, Hindu, Moslem, Buddhist, *anyone*—who loves God above all else and sees Him in everyone and everything. If we save ourselves, each in our own way, we would help save others without trying.

We Are Not Alone

Even though many of us are journeying toward divine awareness, we often feel alone while walking the spiritual path. But we must not lose heart—water does seek its own level, and eventually people who are like-minded magically run into one another. These "chance" encounters inspire our quest for enlightenment because the Holy Spirit's loving presence opens our hearts when we meet in His name.

In addition to our earthly friends, there are also unseen companions, guardian angels that guide and protect us. They help us carry out the Father's will, allowing spirit to manifest in all situations. As the Lord's Prayer directs, "Thy kingdom come, Thy will be done, on earth as it is in heaven." Our unseen friends inspire us to continue on despite all obstacles, even when our humanness resists spiritual guidance. When we overcome a difficult situation or purge some form of ignorance from our beings, we feel the strength of our Christed selves.

As our awareness expands, we may be slow to release old thoughts and behaviors. We must not judge ourselves too harshly when our reluctance to grow causes us to falter temporarily. At these times, we should seek the council of our spirit guides, mentally asking for assistance and then listening carefully for a reply. By quickening our spiritual growth, our unseen brothers and sisters help us awaken the dormant nine-tenths of our potential sleeping within.

We mustn't be afraid to contact our invisible advisors, but we shouldn't be surprised if they contact us first! These loving companions help show us the greater beauty that can be ours forever if we align ourselves with God.

The True Message of Jesus the Christ

Two thousand years ago, Jesus incarnated on the earth plane. A being of pure love, He showed by His resurrection and ascension that through the perfection of love we can achieve immortality. When Jesus said, "*I AM* the way, the truth and the light, and only he who passeth through Me shall reach the kingdom of heaven," He was speaking more generally than literally. Truly, Jesus as wayshower and gatekeeper is responsible for the entry of all souls into the higher realms. However, we need to develop not only our relationship with the "personal Jesus", but with the same Christ Consciousness with which Jesus is united. *Man* has developed the religions originating in the universal truths lived by the Master Jesus; to entertain the notion of eternal damnation if unaligned to these religions limits the boundless, non-dogmatic Cosmic Christ!

Whenever Jesus said the words, "I AM", He was referring to the *Great I AM*, the God-presence found not only in Him, but in everyone, for we are all children of God. This universal force, also known as the Christ Consciousness, is the living God within that helps us climb the ladder of God-Realization. As we make our ascension, everything we think, feel and see affirms our connection to the Messiah who said, "*I AM with you always.*"

Some of us may have visions of Jesus or receive special instructions from Him that help us with our work; but as

World Teacher, He directly or indirectly guides us all regardless of our religious beliefs. Also guiding and instructing us is the legion of Ascended Masters, those beings who have already reached their liberation and freedom in God.

We must follow the teachings of Jesus every day, especially in this time of great ignorance. Jesus simply wants us to love the I AM Presence in each other as He did while on Earth. He said, "Come unto me as a little child," for He wants us to be open-minded, open-hearted and filled with love. Then we will see the Christ Consciousness in everyone.

Many of us believe that accepting Jesus as Savior automatically guarantees us a place in heaven, regardless of how judgmental or hard-hearted we might be; realize this acceptance is only the first step in the initiation to Godhood. Those who see Jesus as Lord but still hold hatred in their hearts will find salvation difficult. We must love *all* our "neighbors", not only those who belong to the same church or follow the same path as we do. Many of us who trumpet our love for Jesus will be shocked when He returns with the legion of Ascended Masters and takes with Him those who have truly *lived* His teachings and not just paid them lip service.

When Jesus said, "I AM the Resurrection and the Life", He invited us to accept the Christ Consciousness. Jesus opens the door to eternal life, but *we* must walk through it by praying, fasting, meditating and acting selflessly; after all, spirituality requires not only observation but participation! As love reveals the mysteries of life, we will begin to see the Christ in everyone.

The Power of the Word

"In the beginning was the Word, and the Word was with God, and the Word was God."

—The Gospel According to Saint John

The Word has many names: the Logos, the Lost Word, Aum, Amen, Oman, I AM and countless others. God's Word is the source of all creation. He made the earth by commanding:

"'Let there be light,' and there was light ... And God said, 'Let the waters under the heavens be gathered together in one place and let the dry lands appear,' and it was so.

... And God said, 'Let the earth bring forth grass, the herb yielding seed and the fruit tree yielding fruit after its kind, whose seed is in itself, upon earth,' and it was so."

—The Book of Genesis

GOD CREATED THE EARTH, heavens, seas, moon and all things by speaking them into being. The Word, or Logos, is the source of all speech, all sound, all manifestation. We can hear God's voice and learn Its secrets if we prepare an inner place where we can receive Its Divine Melody.

To prepare this tabernacle, we must first gain control over our faculty of speech. Though we may not be aware of it, what we say radiates positive or negative energy. Negative comments about ourselves and others limit our world because they limit us. Every time we say "I cannot" or "I will not", we condition ourselves to dwell on the negative. That's why the old saying, "If you can't say anything nice, don't say anything at all" is so powerful. At times unpleasant feelings accumulate and must be expressed, but we should not use words as a weapon intending harm. Any expression may set into motion events or circumstances that could serve to bring that very idea into existence, so we must exercise great care when our expressions are negative. Thus we must use discrimination when we speak, always considering our words beforehand.

It is also important to breathe evenly and rhythmically when speaking so the prana, or life force, will circulate, quieting the mind and calming the emotions. Only when we are calm can we express love through our thoughts and words. Utilizing the breathe will raise our quality of life, freeing us to speak clearly and effortlessly. As we stop misusing the spoken word, we begin to properly use the Logos, the Word of God.

> "...And the Word was made flesh, and dwelt among us, and we beheld His glory: the glory as of the only begotten of the Father, full of grace and truth."
>
> —John 1:14

In many religions, the second person of the Trinity is considered the Word of God. Christians find this in the New Testament, where Christ is often referred to as "the Word". Through the mystery of the incarnation of the Word, man's imperfection and God's perfection inhabit the same form. As man receives the Word, his being becomes more and more filled with the God presence until he is wholly divine. Thus, though Jesus was born of a woman, the Word entered into and was with Him. Gnostic Christians believed that this same Word could enter any man who had sufficiently prepared himself. Interestingly, the Latin word "sonus" became both the English word "son" (meaning child) and the French word "son" (meaning sound). This dual meaning of the Word—both sound and son, both vibration and consciousness—is nowhere more apparent than in the apocryphal poem of the Gospel of St. John. According to David Tame's *The Secret Power of Music*, this work is almost identical to the opening of the biblical Gospel of St. John, except in each case "the Word" is replaced by "Mind"—for example, "In the beginning was Mind."

We can all experience sonship through our Father's cosmic vibration, "the Word". The chanting of the sacred syllable "om" accompanied by deep and rhythmic breathing can help cleanse us and prepare us to receive God's message. In fact, the chanting of any mantra having "om" as its root helps us resonate with the vibration of our Holy Father.

We must always be listening for God's Word, the unstruck sound, for it will enter us when we least expect it. That is how our mysterious Father-Mother God works, for when we have given up the desire for liberation—when we are truly empty—only then are we completely filled with spirit.

> "Do ye seek after the mysteries? No mystery is more excellent saving only *the mystery* of the seven vowels and their *Forty and Nine Powers* and their number thereof; and no name is more excellent than all these vowels. A name wherein be contained all names, all lights, all powers, knowing it, if a man quit this body of matter, no smoke, nor darkness, nor Ruler of the Sphere, or of Fate shall be able to hold back the soul that knoweth that name. If he shall utter that unto the fire, the darkness shall flee away."
>
> —from *The Secret Power Of Music*
> by David Tame

God Is the True Messiah

Recently I was talking with my four year old daughter, Sara. I was saying that she is an angel. With a certainty that belied her age she looked at me and said, "I am nothing." I was about to give her a fatherly lecture on self esteem when the truth of her profound statement penetrated me like a laser beam.

Sara's simple statement is exactly what the game of life is all about. Those few words are precisely what humility, egolessness and stepping aside are all about. Jesus knew this intimately when He came to glorify the Father.

What is a messiah, a savior, a prophet, or a teacher of God but one who allows himself or herself to be "nothing". God can work through us unimpeded in that nothingness. Jesus knew that nothing happens without God; that God and God alone creates, sustains and destroys!

Jesus expressed to me that He never wanted the title of messiah or savior because He knew that it was His Father working through Him who was, is, and always will be the True Messiah. Jesus is the head of the Office of the Christ, and rightly so. He does not want to be seen as Lord or God because He is neither independent of our Father, nor of the Celestial Hierarchy. He is obedient to His Creator and He simply asks that you do likewise.

It saddens Jesus to see how spiritual leaders glorify themselves in the name of Himself and the Father, vainly elevating themselves and forgetting their God. If you are a spiritual leader and you have been seduced by your power and glory, then take an honest look and repent. For the hour of Great Change is upon us. There is no more serious violation of universal law than to lead people and be blinded by spiritual pride and selfrighteousness.

There is no One important in life except our Creator, the Lord God Almighty. And as we prostrate ourselves before the Lord of the Universe, we start to become humbly great in Him again. The Great Change is about remembering the Father who has given and given and given but Who has been continually forgotten.

Many people have said that Jesus failed in His role as the grand ambassador, or the only begotten of the Father. I say just the opposite. Jesus stood, taught, healed and loved as purely as our Father in heaven, for He became one with Him. He said that you also could allow the Father to work through you and even greater things will happen if you would prepare a place to receive God.

This means the inner task shall be easier, though the outer world will go through its metamorphosis. Enter the Peace Train now and watch the true Messiah—God the Father—work His magic through you.

This is the time of the collective "Messiah", the time when mankind as a whole chooses to be chosen. Do not get caught up in titles, spiritual names and egos. Become "nothing", as my little Sara so purely reminded me.

Listen to your children for they have much to tell you. Give praise, thanks and love to the Guru of Gurus, the Lord of Lords, the superbeing we call God. Become like Him. This is Self Realization, Perfection, Mastery, Ascendancy!

Realize that God takes every step and every breath with you. Every heartbeat reverberates as one in Him. So let us see the Messiah in each other and allow our consciousness to be accelerated. Let us prepare the table for the Feast to honor His Son, Jesus. Let us rejoice, for the Hour of Great Change is at hand!

Ascension Is for Everyone

IT IS EVERYONE'S BIRTHRIGHT to ascend to the level of pure spirit! To ascend is to reach the eternal state of man as an individualized presence of God. So many people think that Jesus was the only one to have ascended, yet countless souls before Him and countless others since have done so. Jesus' ascension did make it easier for others to follow Him up the golden ladder of spiritual attainment because He took on part of the world's karmic debt. Everyone can win this victory; why shouldn't each of us aspire to the heights of God-realization?

Everything on this earth fades away; God's domain, our true home, is where we must eventually go. We incarnate on earth in order to learn lessons, work out karma and, if we are ready, proclaim God's work to His children. To some, the task of ascension might seem so remote and arduous that they never try to emulate the likes of Jesus, Buddha, Saint Germain, or the Mother Mary. Yet everyone has the potential to be humbly great in God.

If we acknowledge the God-presence and work steadily each day, we become that on which we focus. The will is supreme; as we direct it, we open ourselves to the Divine Will of the Father. An inner shift stirs our essence from its deep sleep, making us aware of God in all things.

Those who are satisfied by sense pleasures and material gain are only living a partial existence. But the Father is patient, and He waits for His children to rise in spirit and come to Him of their own volition. This journey cannot be forced; we must feel the longing to come home more strongly than anything else. The earth is not our permanent abode, regardless of how many exquisite homes we may have in picturesque locations. Our spiritual home, in the Father's house of many mansions, is ours forever.

Set the goal of ascension in your heart and never waver. You'll experience the ups and downs of your humanness along the way, but keep going. When the time is ripe, when *we* are ripe, God will pluck us from the tree of life. We are His fruit, His creation, His children; when we overflow with love and "at-one-ment" with everything, we will reach a higher expression of ourselves. May we all rise with quiet and steady intensity toward the goal our heart of hearts longs to achieve—to be reunited in God forever.

There Is No Death

THE PURPOSE OF LIFE is to defeat death! Many believe that all there is to life is what we are in body and what we have here on earth. These people live isolated lives, never questioning or confronting their mortality; thus, they give up immortality. Why must we die when the everlasting spirit of God dwells in us all?

Because of the ignorance that permeates the world, most people don't aspire to anything beyond what they perceive through their senses. Those who cling to this limited view have already begun to die of spiritual lethargy. It is our ignorance of God and our enslavement to sense gratification that keep us spinning on the wheel of death and rebirth for incarnation upon incarnation. Of course, most of those who strongly believe in the idea of death reject the idea of reincarnation just as strongly; certain omissions from the Bible that refer to and support the existence of reincarnation notwithstanding. It is time to stop listening to our old tapes of limitation and begin tasting eternal freedom.

The times ahead are going to be ones of great spiritual discovery and, as part of our refinement, a time of great upheaval. If we stand tall in spirit we will not fear or misunderstand the manifestations of this age. *There is no death for the Children of the Light*! Many trials and hardships may await, but as Jesus said, "If you could see your true form (your seamless garment) which came into existence before your physical form, then you would be willing to endure anything." Focus on God, trusting His presence implicitly.

God is a being of total love; do not interpret the coming earth changes as the actions of a vengeful, unforgiving Creator. *This is simply not so!* We have brought about these changes ourselves by not paying enough attention to our spirits and indulging our egos. Each of us must defeat the altered ego or Anti-Christ within—no one can do it for us.

A beautiful discipline to follow is that of *ahimsa*, a Sanskrit term meaning "non-violence in thought, word and deed." This idea was the basis for Mahatma Gandhi's concept of passive resistance, later echoed in the work of Dr. Martin Luther King, Jr. To perfect ahimsa is to become perfect in love; to become perfect in love is to be united with the God-presence. When that occurs, the myth of death will be completely overcome.

We are the Children of the Light, forever alive in God. Let love be our protective shield, let sacred knowledge be our guide and let faith in our Creator be the torch we carry throughout all we must endure.

The Blue Pearl

"O seekers after the knowledge of perfection the very eye of your eye, where the void comes to an end, the Blue Pearl, pure, sparkling radiant, that which opens the center of repose when it arises, is the great place of the conscious Self. Look, my brother, this is the hidden secret of this experience."

Play of Consciousness
Baba Muktananda

"It is always found around the Blue Pearl, and it is said that the radiance of the firmament within the crown chakra comes from the splendor of the *Blue Pearl*. I meditated on it every day, and each day there arose the awareness 'I am the self.' Sometimes I would also see the Blue Pearl moving in and out of the crown chakra for short periods. If you ever have a vision of the coming of a great saint, you should understand that it is all happening through the agency of the Blue Pearl."

Play of Consciousness
Baba Muktananda

AS A STUDENT OF THE GREAT SIDDHA, Baba Muktananda, I was fascinated by the image of the Blue Pearl. Having read about it in Baba's book "Play of Consciousness", I longed to see the Blue Pearl in my meditation. When I first awakened to the Blue Pearl, I found it to be the most beautiful expression of life that I had ever seen.

I could never tire of watching the Blue Pearl, becoming the Blue Pearl, or seeing it perform its play of consciousness. While I worked with other people individually I would observe it coming out of my eye at the speed of light, entering into the person, and exploding in his or her consciousness.

This happens spontaneously to people I see when I am walking in the world. As Baba always stressed, the Blue Pearl is totally independent of its manifestation.

Recently I was speaking with a friend inside the kitchen of his restaurant. It was almost time to close the restaurant; there were hardly any people left. The snow falling outside seemed to bring out the child in us; in no time we were throwing snowballs at each other in the rear entrance of the kitchen. As we ducked the oncoming snowballs it was as if we were eight years old again. All of our roles disappeared in the joy of the moment.

As I was leaving I decided to throw one more snowball at my friend. Just as the snowball caught him in his mid-section, the Blue Pearl followed and exploded in the area of his heart. Little did he know of the gift he was sent by God.

Baba's teacher, Swami Nityananda, recently gave me a great gift—a golden robe—to signify that I had become a Sat-Guru, a teacher of truth. Words cannot express the joy I experienced in receiving this gift, nor my deep appreciation for Baba's great tutelage. Baba himself spoke with me in that experience and said he anticipates our meeting again in the not too distant future. He reiterated that all things are one, all traditions are one and truly East and West are one in God's kingdom. Finally, Baba wished me good luck in my mission. A mission, as he put it, "carrying the light through the winter of mankind's evolution."

Awaken the Dreamer

"Without change something deep inside us sleeps and seldom if ever awakens. The sleeper must awaken."

> From *Dune*, the Movie.
> Book by Frank Herbert

MOST OF US LIE FAST ASLEEP in the self-created night. We are so imbued with our logic and reasoning that the dreamer inside us is prevented from awakening. The Dreamer is synonymous with the Christ or the Spirit of Life. Because we perceive ourselves as the doer, separate from God, from each other, from our higher self and from our higher purpose, the Dreamer remains asleep.

It is time to rouse the sleeper from the night of doubt and disbelief. It is time to shake off the darkness of human logic and rationality. It is time to awaken the Spirit of Love and Unity. We live on the cusp of the Golden Age of Enlightenment, the time of glorious change when all of humanity shall stand as one. Embrace change, for it is the greatest teacher of all. The change we are given by God is given to help us release the skin of the ego-personality in order to awaken Christ Consciousness.

Change is meant to draw from the Real Self the essential qualities of trust and confidence. Its true purpose is to deliver us from fear so that we can live forever in the light of wisdom and freedom. Thus, as we can let go of the old and embrace the new we will shine as beings of light, transformed by the flame of God's refining fire.

Throughout the times of my personal change and adversity, my still small voice would say: "You are not losing, but gaining." To experience change is to be given the opportunity for Self-realization and enlightenment. But one needs to let go of fear in order to experience the fullness of God's abiding love within oneself. I can clearly recall the way the Father spoke to me about this when He said: "When will you trust me completely?"

As every one of us must go through personal change for our betterment, so must our dear Earth mother experience change for her enlightenment. That is why all of us should flow with our Earth mother as she changes her surface to prepare for the New Order. Just as we look forward to the New Jerusalem and the millennia of peace, so does our beloved Earth mother while she cleanses herself from the pain and selfishness of the few; the few who ruined things for the many.

It is time for the many to stand up and throw off the old order of the past. It is time for the multitudes to stand as the Collective Messiah and cast off the sleeper. It is time for us to reclaim our world. The collective apathy and fear must change into fellowship and love.

You will stand in joy and certainty as the dreamer awakens. No longer will you feel as if there are two of you. For you will merge within, and through your God-Self sense no separation within or without. This state of awareness awaits us all, the by-product of both the Earth's changes and our own transformation.

There are certain ways to hasten the process of change. Pray with all your might. Meditate on the source of your being. Find the stillness that silences the discordant promptings of logic and reasoning.

As you play your part and as you discover the real you in you, all the walls of separation will dissolve before your eyes. As you remember who you are, and as you rest in that remembrance, you will see your Self in everyone and everything. This is our "Hope for Deliverance" that Paul McCartney sings about so beautifully. This divine spark, this light in the sleeper, waits to be delivered from the darkness that surrounds us.

You must ask for that deliverance. Do not expect someone to do it for you. *You* must knock; then the door will open. *You* must ask; then it will be given to you.

Persevere with yourself. It takes time to eliminate every particle of duality; duality is a myth of the collective unconscious. Be patient. Be constant. Above all, love yourself as you are. Then the sleeper can awaken. Then all of us can stand as one.

We Are the Heroes We Are Looking For

We all need heroes to inspire us. We naturally set them on pedestals, placing them higher than we perceive ourselves to be. In sports, entertainment, literature, spirituality and other fields of endeavor, we have all had heroes who could do no wrong in our eyes. We can gain much inspiration from these souls; their examples can give us the courage to persist and grow. It is important to keep our hero-worship in perspective, however. Each heroic example only helps to illustrate that the capacity for greatness exists in everyone if we but believe in ourselves. We all have a source of strength, courage and wisdom that should be honored.

The hero we are looking for exists within us as ourselves—not as the ego self, but as the Divine Self. This Divine Self is found equally in everyone and everything, and is our source of life. Often people shy away from spirituality; the notion of God seems remote and abstract, and the universe so vast, that we are made to feel small by comparison. *How untrue this is*! Let us worship the one true hero worthy of all praise, the Father-Mother God, who exists within as the source of life itself. It is said that life is its own reward. With God at the center of our lives, there is no limit to what we can attain individually and collectively.

Great souls such as Jesus, Buddha and Lao Tsu did not take the credit for their accomplishments, choosing instead to direct the praise to their Creator. Any holy man or woman is simply a way-shower guiding us to our inner selves. For heaven's sake, we must be courageous and have faith in our divine natures!

Each of us is a microcosm of the universe. God has truly made us in His image, giving us all the attributes of perfection. There is a story told of a prospector who searched for gold his whole life. He looked everywhere—by hill, valley and stream—and he asked everyone he met to help him look for his treasure. Sadly, he passed on without finding any gold. His friends decided to bury him under the house he'd lived in his whole life; as they dug his grave, they discovered a vein of gold the likes of which had never been seen. And so it is with us; when we look for our spiritual gold everywhere but within, we will never find it. Each of us is at the end of a spiritual rainbow; each of us has a pot of gold within—God. All our heroes, each with his or her own "gold" fall short, for we must ultimately acknowledge only the God-Self that we uniquely are.

This is why Jesus gave the commandments to "love the Lord thy God with all thy heart, strength and mind," and "love thy neighbor as thyself." We should remember these every day of our lives and watch our heroes, the Divine Beings within each of us, light the way for us and all our brothers and sisters. Once this light begins to shine, neither we nor our world will ever be the same. Our greatest joy will be to awaken the hero within our fellow man. In this way, we will help bring the great day of the Lord closer, the day when we all can rest in joy and peace.

We Are the Collective Messiah

THE *COLLECTIVE MESSIAH* is a concept that must be understood and implemented *now*! What is, or more accurately who are the Collective Messiah? By the covenant God has made with us, *we His children* are His torch-bearers in this period of great change. Each of us must do his or her part, large and small, for many hands are needed to raise world consciousness in preparation for the coming of the heavenly Messiah at the end of this, the age of the Holy Spirit.

This Messianic work has already begun, producing movies such as *Star Wars*, *E.T.*, *Working Girl*, *Field of Dreams*, *Close Encounters of the Third Kind*, *Cocoon*, *Willow*, *Ghost* and songs such as "Let The River Run" (the theme song of *Working Girl*), "We Are The World" and "Higher Love", among others. These and many other spiritually and socially conscious works are helping to raise the vibration of mankind. Remember, there are emissaries of light in every walk of life, silently playing their parts in this grand play!

What can we, the common people, do to align ourselves with this program of change? We can listen attentively to the Christ Consciousness within and closely follow the leadership of our spirits. We are one with Jesus and the Ascended Masters, united in the consciousness we share. By living spiritually aware lives, we can cleanse the atmosphere surrounding us, helping our brothers and sisters in the process.

As each soul comes closer to achieving his or her potential in God, the day of humanity's collective graduation draws near.

As the wayshower, Jesus demonstrated what each of us is capable of doing if we open our hearts to what we truly are. As He emphasized, "Empty yourself and be filled with the Holy Spirit." The kingdom of heaven is within us all! Through Jesus' ministry, the portals of the heavens were opened; He paved the way for us to do even greater work than He, and to follow Him to heaven in Ascension if we are worthy.

The work we do each day is very important, more so than we realize. We can't leave everything for the handful of souls chosen to be God's messengers; we are *all* His messengers, each in our own way. This world won't move from the third to the fifth dimension while we stand idly by; *we all must do our part*! By manifesting the gifts of prophecy, healing, leadership and service through the Holy Spirit, and by helping our neighbors rise above their fears of the Apocalypse, we will fulfill the role of Collective Messiah. Let us witness the bringing of the heavens onto the earth!

The Proper Application of the Great I AM

THE GREAT I AM of God is the energy animating our lives. Few of us acknowledge this fact; we can be so absorbed in the outer world of our senses, we don't see the God-Self within. If we did, we'd realize that all the secrets of heaven and eternity are found in the I AM Consciousness.

To make this realization, it is essential to positively affirm our existence in God. Whenever we begin a statement with the words "I AM", or simply "I", we should make the rest of the declaration positive in nature. To use the I AM Consciousness negatively in statements such as "I AM too fat," "I AM not good-looking," "I AM not smart enough" or "I AM not spiritual" is a mis-use of God-energy and brings negative results. God supplies the raw materials—the world we live in and the means to live in it—while we determine how these resources are put to use. Only positive commands yield positive results!

Instead of wallowing in negativity and misusing God's power, we can create paradise on earth with the positive intentions of our thoughts, words and actions. If we say "God I AM," "I AM the focused breath of my being, bringing harmony into my world" or "I AM the wealth of God made available to me in this moment," positive, God-directed outcomes must result—that is the nature of universal law. Give these affirmations a try; have faith and persist, for they will only be as effective as our belief in them and our diligence in their use.

As our lives are brought into balance and our quest for enlightenment intensifies, we can use the statements Jesus used to hasten His ascension: *"I AM the resurrection and the life,"* *"I AM the open door that no man may shut,"* and *"I AM the light of the world."* Since Jesus blazed a path for us all to follow, these statements are for everyone to use; their utterance is not blasphemy against God, but a profession of oneness with Him. Remember, Jesus Himself urged His disciples to fully utilize the God-Presence within when He told them, "Even greater works shall ye do because I go to My Father's house."

Positive declarations using the Great I AM unify us in spirit as they break the chains binding us. Through strong conviction grounded in humility, we can activate the I AM Presence within. When this occurs, nothing and no one can keep us from the freedom we are destined to experience. Use these affirmations, God's gifts to us, until the final victory is won.

How to Protect Yourself from Negativity

As we approach the Omega—the end of time—and the subsequent new beginning, we must be cognizant of the work of the dark brotherhood and its many faces. It is extremely important to recognize and be able to neutralize the negative forces within and around us.

Some representatives of darkness are negative disembodied spirits, dark forces and dark or fallen angels. There are people who have lived and died, yet their spirits remain earthbound due to strong earthly desires and attachments; these are known as disembodied spirits. While not always negative, many are depressed, jealous and confused due to the difficulties of their lives while embodied and their subsequent reluctance to return to the light.

These spirits can be found anywhere but seem to congregate in areas like hospitals and bars, though in each for a different reason. In hospitals, many patients pass away during their stays, and many of their spirits cling to the earth plane, not wanting to travel onward . Thus large numbers of disembodied spirits can be present. The negativity of these spirits leads them to negative environments; bars are particularly desirable, with their large crowds of alcohol-consuming people. These confused spirits, unbeknownst to us, can enter through holes in our auras, holes made larger by alcohol and drug consumption. Once inside, they steal our peace and disturb our emotional states; these spirits want to continue "living", and they will do so—vicariously, through us—if we allow it.

Our first defense against disembodied spirits is to detect their presence in us. This can be difficult, since the "voice" of such a spirit can sound like the voice of the lower mind, or even the Higher Mind. If we are attuned to our inner voices, we can usually tell the difference between our inner voices and any foreign voice; we may simply sense that something isn't quite right.

If we have attracted a disembodied spirit or spirits, we shouldn't feel ashamed or blame ourselves. These spirits are an arbitrary part of the confusion existing on the earth plane; in this time of great change, the realm of darkness is desperate. We, for our part, must be aware of these spirits and work through God to counteract them.

Dark forces are beings sent with a specific purpose—to undermine a certain task, or to seed separation and discord among people of the light. They can attack psychically and even physically; our one true defense lies in remembering and reinforcing the unity of being and the clarity of purpose we find in God.

Dark or fallen angels can be incarnate or discarnate; the earth and surrounding lower heavens are their homes, since the higher heavens have been purged of all dark forces. At this time, the earth and its surrounding atmosphere need to be cleansed as well; as these dark angels gather against the forces of light, the battle lines are being drawn, and such a cleansing will eventually result. The Children of the Light will be these dark angels' targets, subtly or overtly feeling their sting. This clash must occur; the Sons and Daughters of the Light must battle darkness so light can enjoy its final triumph.

Lightbearers, *do not be afraid*—remain calm and know that *knowledge is power*! We must realize that each of us is protected by God; there is no further need to avoid the tasks at hand. We should embrace them wholeheartedly, for in the heart of God, nothing can touch us. Then we can relinquish the fear that weakens our armors of light!

One way to clear any and all of these forces is by invoking this command: "By the power of the Ascended Jesus Christ, I (AM) dissolve and disintegrate all disembodied spirits, all negative entities, all negative thoughtforms, all dark angels, all dark forces, all dark psychic forces, all detrimental planetary influences and everything pertaining to or having its root in darkness or evil by the power of the Ascended Jesus Christ and the Ascended Host, *Amen*." We can clear ourselves of dark forces by using this command, or clear an area, such as a room or house, by walking through this area repeating it. While using this invocation, know that the "*Universal I*" is speaking, not just the "individual I".

The most powerful mantra or saying we can repeat is the Hebrew phrase, "*Kodoish, Kodoish, Kodoish, Adonai Sabayoth.*" This phrase, which is continuously sung at the throne of the Father, translates in English to, "Holy, Holy, Holy is the Lord God of Hosts." This supreme salutation can help us discern between those of the light and those of darkness masquerading as light. If any entity wants to take our spirits for an out-of-body journey, we should invoke this phrase. If the entity is of darkness, it must identify itself as such or be destroyed—such is the power of this mantra. It should be repeated many times, for it will align our energies with those of God's throne. Remember, this is a *universal* salutation; it can and should be used by anyone regardless of religious affiliation.

Another very powerful mantra in the Indian *Om Namah Shivaya*. It means, "I bow to that consciousness (God) which is the source of all life." *Om* resides in the upper space, and the sounds *Na, Mah, Shi, Va,* and *Ya* are the sounds representative of the first five chakras. So the chanting of this mantra acts to quicken the vibration of your chakras by balancing them through the agency of sound. The sounds act like a cellular tuning fork bringing everything into harmony. I learned firsthand of the power of this great mantra. I would use it to clear myself when seeing people in sessions because invariably they would drop off their old baggage (disembodied spirits similar to what Whoppi Goldberg's character experienced in the movie *Ghost* after she was really doing the works). I had a friend from California who would assist by removing them with scientific equipment. She would then help them by encouraging them to go into the light so they no longer would be a nuisance to people on the Earth. This particular time she was assisting me, I decided to do it on my own because of a miscommunication. So in the car I chanted *Om Namah Shivaya* very powerfully and lovingly on my way to a movie. Later that evening she called back to question what had happened since when she went to assist me there was nothing to remove. She, being of a more scientific persuasion, was both curious and astounded by the power of this mantra. In retrospect I know these events unfolded as they did to give proof positive to the effectiveness of these sacred syllables. Don't be frightened by the suggestion of disembodied entities or any forces mentioned previously. They simply are part of the unseen world which comprises 97% of our existence. The great Indian Saint Babaji, the teacher of Paramahansa Yogananda's teacher and guide to Jesus while he was in India, said that *Om Namah Shivaya* has the power of 10,000 *hydrogen bombs*. May we all use this great Gift of God to bless, heal, prosper, and protect our dear Earth Mother.

We must invoke these commands and mantras *daily*—they are supremely useful gifts from God that merit diligent and tenacious use. We don't have to *be*ware of life if we are fully *a*ware of our lives in God. With this knowledge, we can guard against the forces of darkness and negativity seeking to undermine our missions in life.

OM Shanti, Shanti, Shanti!

We Are the Conduits of God's Power

As we move into this age of tremendous challenge, it is important to remember the lessons not learned by previous civilizations on the continents of Atlantis and Lemuria. Many of us were incarnate then and abused the powers with which we were entrusted; as a result, both societies simply disappeared from the face of the earth in the blink of an eye!

As Children of the Light, we are being given another opportunity to bring forth a Golden Age of high spiritual consciousness. However, *this* time we must understand it is the power of God moving through us that gives us the love, knowledge and strength to handle all circumstances. We must make the same realization as Jesus and other masters did—that of ourselves we can do nothing. Yes, *we must each humbly claim our Divine Right, acknowledging ourselves as channels of God's energy.*

By selflessly living under the Law of the One, we will all work together for the benefit of the whole. Thankfulness and appreciation shall be our motto; sharing and giving from the heart shall be the law of the land.

We who truly love God are on the precipice of something wonderful; let us remember the mistakes of Atlantis and Lemuria and not repeat them. It's time to join together as one family, with one heart and one mind, and welcome in a new and brighter tomorrow. May we all stay true to our Higher Selves, playing our parts to usher in the Glory of Glories. Amen.

The Law of One

THE LAW OF ONE, which states there is only one energy uniting us all as one people, is the most basic yet profound universal law. We are truly *one*, and every word or deed is an expression and extension of the one energy that sustains our lives—God.

Unfortunately, we are a people unaware of our unity; our ignorance has resulted in a divided world filled with war and chaos. My brothers and sisters, when we kill our fellow man we are killing ourselves; when we hate a people for racial, religious or political reasons we are hating a part of ourselves; when we foster negative feelings we are hurting the whole and, therefore, ourselves. Look at the selfish choices we have made; is there no end to our abuse of the Father's gift of free will?

Man's egocentricity will soon bring yet more agony, for we are in the Omega, the end of times; we have no one to blame but ourselves and must now atone for our loss of spiritual direction. The ego is so strong a presence on the earth plane that it will take many painful steps to turn our attention back to the primary reason for living—to serve and glorify God. Thus, we should try to see this action as a necessary cleansing that must be completed before we can express our souls' intent and truly live as one mind, one heart, one being.

The closer we follow the Law of One, the fewer trials we will undergo before being truly prepared to taste the rapture of the coming Golden Age. As a means to this end, may we step aside from egotism, dogma, political pride and other such belief systems, letting our unified beam of light heal the world in its darkest hour. *We* will determine what we must go through; no matter what comes to pass we must courageously and faithfully uphold God's Law as one people under His loving care.

A Voice Crying in the Wilderness

I AM THE VOICE crying in the wilderness to all mankind to make straight their pathways to God through the Holy Ghost. The hour will soon arrive when the earth will tremble. Fierce winds will blow and bring an end to the old order. Then the beginning of the New Order will be summoned. The Golden Age of love, peace, brotherhood and enlightenment for all.

I am the voice sent by our Father to help point the way home. It is time to put away your toys! It is time to put away your fears! It is time to shake off the lassitude and the inertia of the flesh.

It is time to trust and to listen to our Creator in a way that we have not listened before. The day of reckoning is at hand. But let it not be one of dread. Rather, let it be one of faith and hopefulness. Our Father is a *benevolent and loving benefactor*. Remember always to trust in God's benevolence toward mankind. God loves us all. Unconditionally.

I pray that you open your heart and your mind to the Father. Develop a stronger relationship with God now in these moments of calm before the storm. Let your mind and heart be peaceful.

Remember silence, for it is your greatest ally. In stillness you can hear the voice of the divine communicate guidance to you directly. God is not only inside us but all around us.

The illusion of separateness is a projection of the altered ego. The sense of otherness and aloneness, the feeling of isolation, are the doing of the Anti-Christ in one's human reasoning.

Do not be afraid to take your stand. Listen to your promptings. Stay close to the voice of reassurance that always inspires you to move forward despite the odds. Your duty is to serve God and to please only God.

Prepare yourself for the coming of the New Jerusalem, for all who have ears to hear and eyes to see will in truth know and live in a land of milk and honey, the Kingdom of God on Earth.

God Is Ecstasy

A<small>LTHOUGH IT MAY SEEM IMPORTANT</small> to focus on earth changes and the various adjustments in one's physical life, the most important shift is in the collective consciousness.

Mother Earth and all of her inhabitants who "choose to be chosen" are undergoing the greatest changes. As we open our hearts to our Creator, we are able to put on the garment of light. And when we open ourselves to God we feel the purist joy imaginable. Follow that joy and bliss. As Joseph Campbell has said: "Follow the ecstasy that only serving God can give you."

The Almighty Father is your temple, your sanctuary, your true home. Open and trust Him completely, for then He can move you gloriously in all His ways. Remember, nothing happens without God. He is the animating power behind all life, so give credit where credit is due. Our most sacred duty is the glorification of God. Do not forget that obedience and humility will truly keep you on the straight and narrow road home to Everlasting Life.

You will know the reality of these words because you will begin to experience God directly in your own life. The Ecstasies are so powerful you will not have to wonder if it is indeed true. You will see the veil of illusion lift slowly and gently before your very eyes. You will watch the old human you disappear as God finds a home in you, His child.

Speaking with me directly, the Father has said He wishes that all of His children would open their hearts and minds to

Him. We all have a job to do in the time of The Quickening. Our job is to pray, meditate on God and simplify our lives so that we can hear His voice and His direction. As we follow this direction there will come Love, Ecstasy, Wisdom and Power. My dear friends, we could not have a better boss. Consider how an earthly boss would tolerate the nonsense we place in God's direction. He is the Guru of Gurus, the Light of Lights, the Intelligence moving everything and the Love holding everything in its place. Contemplate this!

As the world trembles, turns and moves into its new cycle, take your attention away from the nonsense of sensory life. Open yourself in prayer and meditation to the Almighty One. When you firmly establish this relationship, all things become possible for you. And as the magic of life reveals itself to you, walk humbly and say thanks to God and the Host of Light.

We are all in this together. There is no separation! When you stop looking toward the outer world for your solace and truly look within yourself, you will perceive the Almighty Lord looking back at you. Honor yourself. Respect yourself. Kneel to your Self, for God dwells within you as you!

The Quickening and Activation of Critical Mass

WE ARE LIVING IN THE TIME of accelerated change that is referred to as "the Quickening." The "Quickening" will cause those who choose to be chosen to expand beyond the boundaries of our human comprehension. Realize that all things come from God the Father—the superbeing who is the source of all life. God wishes that you allow Him to pour His Love, Wisdom and Power through you so that you can experience this "Quickening."

There is no separation between heaven and earth; it is only one's mind and conditioning that see these things as such. In truth, when you open yourself to God's radiation, you will see life in an entirely different light - God's light. There is absolutely nothing that exists without God's presence. Not one square inch of creation. But humankind has been caught in its own collective web, unable to free itself from its self-created night. Make your peace with your Creator now, in this year of grace, as the earth begins to cleanse itself of man's wrongdoings. God eagerly awaits the return of His Creation, for He loves it with an unconditional heart.

I pray that all who read these words will connect their hearts back to their higher power - God - and truly repent. I am but a messenger sent to help you help yourselves. Just as I have been enlightened and instructed by God and the Host of Light regarding the extent of my service to mankind, so I encourage you to open your heart to God who will walk with you and instruct you every step of the way.

Cast aside your doubts, your worries and your fears. God alone is real. He has expressed to me that "Man has suffered long enough." The "Quickening" is upon us. We are to institute the "New Jerusalem."

As you open your heart to God, your life will change dramatically. You will become more aware of the spiritualizing work being done on you while you are in your sleeping state. The more quickly you surrender, the sooner you can drink of the River of Life.

Trust your Creator. Have faith in Him and allow Him to work His "Magic" through you. Remember, humility and obedience are the keys to successfully climbing Jacob's Ladder. As God commands, obey with great dignity and love. The "Quickening" is for the benefit of all, though many will not open their minds and hearts to see it as such.

If you take the time to pray and meditate on God, all these truths will be self-evident. God in His greatness gives you the choice to say "yes" or to say "no." I pray that you will say "yes" to the "Quickening" for we are all one heartbeat in God forever and ever. And as that heartbeat becomes stronger and stronger we will approach "critical mass." Critical mass is achieved when 51% or more of the population is united in spirit. That is to say we are one in Love, Wisdom, and Power despite the fact that we may travel down different tributaries to reach the same ocean or source. As the force of this divine love energy gains dominion over the planet, the remaining 49% will be pulled through by the collective effect of this new consciousness.

I pray with all of my heart that we change the collective consciousness from fear, hatred, and violence to that of Love and the Law of One. In this way the "New Jerusalem" can be instituted more softly and gently, thereby not necessitating Mother Nature's manifestation of natural cataclysms to produce her healing. I know that spark exists in more than half the population. I therefore dedicate my life to bring about the activation of this reality and hope that all who read this will do likewise. Through the power of collective thought, collective energy, collective love and collective action anything is possible. There is always hope! Let's do it together!

All of the so-called "little people" in the world must make their presences felt. The dishwashers, cabbies, nurses, policemen, firefighters, farmers, etc., must claim their *God dominion* and take their places as the *collective messiah*. This collective love force will transform individuals, who intern will light others' lamps by their example and their essences. This is the *domino effect* which is all a part of "critical mass." Remember there are no "little people" in God's eyes, and everyone's task is necessary and important to the "Great Work." Find your place in the circle of life by taking your stand! Let peace, freedom and love reign supreme upon this planet, and may the "New Jerusalem" come quickly and gently, Amen.

"*That which is not given is lost forever.*"

City of Joy (the movie)

Epilogue

We have the greatest of all challenges before us. A destiny of such joy, peace, and grandeur beckons to each and everyone of us. As children of the most high living God, we need look no further than our own hearts. We all know the revelation of St. John the Divine to be real and true. That being so, will we as offspring of the Ancient One join as one and hear the clarion call? Or does our collective apathy and sense of materialistic otherness create the same fate that we endured in Lemuria and Atlantis? Remember and let us learn from our past mistakes! It is time for our sense of humanity and spiritual consciousness to override our sense of technological insatiability.

The truth is so simple that we pass it by each and every day and never know that we have done so. We exist as one people, one heart, one energy, and one mind in God. And as one people we can bring the *New Jerusalem* into existence by our thought, feeling, speech, and actions. Simply put, we need to exalt the heart above every other faculty that exists within our consciousness. As God lovingly commanded me to *Teach My Children to Trust the Living God that Lives Inside of Their Hearts* at the entrance to the Great Pyramid in Giza, so I impart this to you. Learn to get still and quiet enough to hear your still small voice which is your connection with the Divine.

The implementation of the *New Jerusalem*, the New Golden Age of peace and enlightenment for all, can be swift and easy depending on everyone's commitment to truth and freedom.

With over 90% of the population believing in God, isn't it time for our overwhelming majority to give the direction to our beleaguered planet? She (Earth Mother) awaits our conscious direction. Our collective destinies lie in our trembling hands of Love or Fear. Which will we pick? I pray with all of my heart that it will be one of Love. We are living in the best of times or the worst of times depending on whether you are attuned to your soul or to your ego-based personality. Be not afraid to make the change. God is one of Love, Mercy, and Forgiveness and will render your personal slate null and void. So don't place the limitations of your personality onto the unconditional Love that your Creator has for you.

Let us focus as one heart, as one people, as one energy and create the dawning of the new tomorrow we all dream about. It takes the conviction of all of our hearts to beat as one and create the world we deserve. Our differences, apathy, and sense of self-righteousness must be replaced by that of Selfless Love, compassion, wisdom, and power. We all have the scepter of dominion at our command to collectively and individually use to bless, heal, prosper, and enlighten ourselves and our fellows. May we visualize the New Jerusalem promised to us by our Creator to come smoothly and swiftly by raising and rising into oneness and unity so that we may act as one mighty army of God. Amen.

To dream the impossible dream,
To fight the unbeatable foe,
To bear with unbearable sorrow,
To run where the brave dare not go.

To right the unrightable wrong,
To love pure and chaste from afar,
To try when your arms are to weary,
To reach the unreachable star.

This is my quest, to follow that star,
No matter how hopeless, no matter how far;
To fight for the right without question or pause,

To be willing to march into hell for a heavenly cause!
And I know, if I'll only be true, to this glorious quest,
That my heart will lie peaceful and calm
When I'm laid to my rest.

And the world will be better for this;
That one man, scorned and covered with scars,
Still strove with his last ounce of courage,
To reach the unreachable stars.

(Till united, all one, we are!)

—"The Impossible Dream"
Words by Joe Darion
Music by Mitch Leigh